...Our Homeland Churches and how to Study Them

OUR HOMELAND
CHURCHES AND
HOW TO STUDY THEM

THE
HOMELAND POCKET BOOKS.

Uniform with this Volume.

No. 1.—NORTH-WEST NORFOLK: From Hunstanton to Cley-next-the-Sea (Nelson's Homeland). By James Hooper. With numerous illustrations from drawings by Walter Dexter, R.B.A. 2/6 net.

No. 2.—A MAP OF THE THAMES FROM OXFORD TO RICHMOND. Scale one inch to the mile. By William Stanford. Letterpress by Arthur Henry Anderson. 1/- net.

No. 3.—NORTH DEVON WITH WEST SOMERSET. By Beatrice and Gordon Home. With numerous illustrations from drawings by Gordon Home and from photographs. 2/6 net.

No. 4.—THE PILGRIMS' ROAD: A practical guide for the pedestrian on the ancient way from Winchester to Canterbury. By Frank C. Elliston-Erwood. With numerous sketch maps, and many illustrations from drawings and photographs. 2/6 net.

Ockham, Surrey.

A rare instance of seven graded lancets.

No. 5.

THE HOMELAND POCKET BOOKS

EDITED BY

PRESCOTT ROW AND ARTHUR HENRY ANDERSON.

OUR HOMELAND CHURCHES AND HOW TO STUDY THEM

By SIDNEY HEATH

WITH MANY ILLUSTRATIONS FROM
DRAWINGS BY J. R. LEATHART AND
OTHERS AND FROM PHOTOGRAPHS

THE HOMELAND ASSOCIATION, LTD.,

For the Encouragement of Touring in Great Britain,

CHANDOS CHAMBERS, 15 BEDFORD STREET, STRAND, LONDON, W.C.

FREDERICK WARNE & CO.

LONDON.   NEW YORK.

A COMPANION volume dealing with Our Homeland Cathedrals is in preparation, and will be published in the autumn of 1912.

A lecture on the subject of this book, "Our Homeland Churches and how to study them," has been prepared, illustrated by a series of beautiful lantern slides. Arrangements can be made for its delivery by competent lecturers, or for the loan or sale of slides. For particulars see page 199.

CONTENTS.

LIST OF ILLUSTRATIONS.

(The illustrations, except those printed in the text, *face* the pages indicated).

Illustrations facing pages 21, 44, 48, 49 53, 55, 58, 60, 61, 65, 66, 69, 71, 75, 76, 77, 80, 81, 83, 86, 152, 153, 155, are reproduced from drawings by Mr. J. R. Leathart; and thanks are due to Mr. Francis Bond, M A., F.G.S., for permission to reproduce, facing page 106, photographs of the fonts at Deerhurst (by G. G. Buckley), Snape (by G. C. Druce), and Roche (by W. H. Walford); of font covers at Trunch (by T. M. Birdseye), and Sudbury St. Peter facing page 107; and of screens at Kenton (by F. H. Crossley) and Barningham, facing page 102; also to Mr. Edward Yates for the two illustrations of St. Stephen, Walbrook, facing page 87.

NOTE : The numbers which appear in parenthesis in the text refer to the page upon or opposite to which an illustration of the special subject or detail will be found.

PREFACE TO SECOND EDITION.

THE first edition of this book was published in 1907, and though, like most books on large subjects, it had its shortcomings, it met with favourable reception at the hands of some thousands of readers, many of whom have been kind enough to express their appreciation in warm terms. Though the edition was a large one, it has been out of print for some time.

In presenting a second edition, the author and editors desire to say that the text has been very largely re-written and extended, and in this work they have had the benefit of kind critical help from many correspondents. Their number is far too great to permit of acknowledgment in detail, but it may at least be stated that they include some of the best authorities in England on various branches of the subject They would, however, specially thank the Rev. Robert A. Davis for various suggestions and additions; also for reading the proofs, for assisting in the compilation of the Glossary, for contributing Appendixes B and D, and for indexing the whole book.

The illustrations have also been almost entirely re-cast, and the author and editors have to express their gratitude for the collaboration in this work of Mr. J. R. Leathart, whose charming series of explanatory drawings will, it is believed, be a very great help to the reader.

In spite of the care given to the production, it is hardly possible that it should be free from errors of fact or discrepancies. The notification of any such will be welcomed, with a view to the improvement of future editions.

PERIODS OF ARCHITECTURE.

Most books and articles dealing either with individual buildings or with architecture, speak of "styles" of English architecture. This division into styles or periods, although not without its disadvantages, is in some respects so convenient that it may be useful to give the names and dates of the so-called styles here.

The periods have been classified by Thomas Rickman (an early authority) as shown below. It should be borne in mind that in each of the tables quoted the dates given are more or less approximate, because each style merged by slow degrees into the next. For further treatment of this subject see page 28.

see page 28.

RICKMAN'S CLASSIFICATION.

Norman :—William I to Stephen, 1066-1154.
Transition Norman :—Henry II, 1154-1189.
Early English Gothic :—Richard I to Henry III, 1189-1272.
Decorated :—Edward I, II, III, 1272-1377.
Perpendicular :—Richard II to Henry VII, 1377-1485.
Tudor :—Henry VIII to Elizabeth, 1485-1600.

Mr. Edmund Sharpe gives seven periods of English architecture up to the time of the Reformation, and dates them as follows :—

ROMANESQUE.

I.	Saxon	from	— to 1066.	
II.	Norman	,,	1066 to 1145	79 years.
III.	Transitional	,,	1145 to 1190	45 ,,

GOTHIC.

IV.	Lancet	from	1190 to 1245	55 years.
V.	Geometrical	,,	1245 to 1315	70 ,,
VI	Curvilinear	,,	1315 to 1360	45 ,,
VII.	Rectilinear	,,	1360 to 1550	190 ,,

As applied to the development of windows alone, these terms Lancet, Decorated, Geometrical, Curvilinear, Perpendicular, are most useful and correct.

OUR HOMELAND CHURCHES

AND HOW TO STUDY THEM.

Chapter I.

Introductory.

HOWEVER much ecclesiologists may differ with regard to the date of the introduction of Christianity
into these islands, and fail to agree as to who was
the first missionary, there is no reason to doubt
that the pagan or pre-Christian religions were not
easily displaced by the tenets of the new faith.
Pope Leo the Great relates that even in his day
the people, when ascending the steps of St. Peter's,
were " wont to turn and make their obeisance to
the sun." If such a thing could happen before the
famous basilica of the great city of Rome, the
scene of so many martyrdoms, and the grave of
so many saints, it requires but little imagination
to picture the difficulties that beset the early
emissaries of the Christian faith in our own land.

Christianity was very far indeed from being
the cause of a continuous and progressive over-
throw of the older cults, and it apparently even
disappeared with the relapse of the populace into
heathenism. In this land, when the Anglo-
Saxons invaded it, Kent and Essex were swept

by a flood of paganism, and Mercia, under
Penda, remained pagan until 633. Bede states
that up to the time of Wilfrid's mission in
681 " all in the province of the South Saxons
were strangers to the name and faith of God."
As the new faith made converts its contest with the
old beliefs grew fiercer, for the mutual antipathy
of hostile creeds is, in itself, accountable for the
persecution by the early Christians. An edict of
Theodoric A.D. 500, directs that all persons found
sacrificing according to pagan rites, shall be put to
death ; and although this and similar edicts were
enforced at intervals, with great cruelty, the policy
adopted by the Church was generally one better
calculated to succeed. It learned, in this country
at any rate, to prefer gradual advance to speedy
conquest, aware that by the former its establishment would be a lasting one, and was pleased
to satisfy its conscience with compromise. If one
thing stands out more clearly than another in the
history of the early struggles of Christianity in this
land, it is that the key-note of the success which
eventually attended the efforts of the missionaries,
is summed up in the word compromise. A politic
regard for popular feeling as associated with long-
standing customs, led the authorities to permit,
and even to sanction, many of the formalities of
unvarnished paganism.

Among the Teutonic nations especially there
was a disposition on the part of the Church to leave

many heathen usages unchallenged, or to asso-
ciate them with Christian doctrine. The early
missionaries had not so much to create new rules
of conduct as to direct the significance attaching
to the old ones into a channel of Christian thought.

And what evidence have we that this spirit of
compromise entered so largely into the efforts of
the early pioneers to engraft the Christian religion
on to a pagan stock ? We have the letter of Pope
Gregory to his bishop Mellitus, given in Bede,
in which the bishop is directed to retain the old
temples and consecrate them, " that the nation,
seeing their temples are not destroyed, may remove
error from their hearts, and knowing and adoring
the true God, may the more familiarly resort to
the place to which they have been accustomed."

And further, the pagan feasts were to be turned
to the honour of God, " to the end that while some
gratifications are outwardly permitted them, they
may the more easily consent to the inward con-
solations of the grace of God, for there is no doubt
that it is impossible to efface everything at once
from their obdurate minds." The policy directed
by the great Pope Gregory and carried out by
Bishop Mellitus and his contemporaries, was, in
brief, to make the transition from pagan error to
Divine truth as little violent as possible. Thus in
England the people would be gathered together in
the places they and their forefathers had long
held sacred—within the stone circle, in the leafy

grove, on the swelling mound, by hoary rock or holy well. And we have evidence of it in stones, once sacred to the rites of pagan worship, being marked with a cross; in wells of water, once sanctified by heathen ceremonies, placed under saintly invocation by Christian feeling; in old church sites whereon Odin and Frigga, and before them Jupiter and Venus, were worshipped.

In dealing with the introduction of Christianity into this country the task would be much simplified if the name of the first missionary could be stated with certainty. Legend and conjecture have been busy for years—to no purpose—concerning the apostle of Britain, for we do not know, and it is highly improbable that we ever shall know, to whom the honour belongs. The beautiful legends of St. Joseph of Arimathea and the Holy Grail, together with the tradition of the wattled church at Glastonbury, are ancient enough if they could be supported by historical evidence and the same may be said about the reputed visits to British shores of the great saints, Peter and Paul. Pure conjecture for the most part are all these various theories, for the lessons to be learned from the architectural remains are insufficient to enable students to dispel the veil of mystery that hangs over the earliest days of British Christianity. We have a few fragments of Roman work in the Christian churches of St. Pancras and St. Martin, at Canterbury; and possibly at Reculver and Lyminge

in Kent, and at Brixworth near Northampton ;
while the foundation-masonry of the little basilican
church at Silchester in Hampshire is perhaps, from
some points of view, the most important of them
all.

Beneath the chancel floor of Lady St. Mary
Church, at Wareham, Dorset, some inscribed stones
were found a few years ago, which that learned
student of pre-Conquest architecture, the Bishop of
Bristol, states most emphatically to be portions of
an old Roman altar, which, although not conclusive,
is presumptive evidence that the present church
stands on the site of a Roman temple.

Such slight evidence as we possess goes to show
that there were Christians in Roman Britain, and
that the British Church continued to advance,
as we find that three British bishops were present
at the Council of Arles in 314. We have also a
few records of pilgrimages made to Rome by the
early British Christians, such as those of Ced-
walla, and of Ine the greatest of English kings before
Alfred, who was the most distinguished of the band
of pilgrims ; and there is always the tradition
of the martyrdom of St. Alban.

Before the coming of the Anglo-Saxons the
Church seems to have established here and there a
firm hold on the people, who held tenaciously to their
possessions, both secular and religious, which were
only wrested from them after a severe struggle.
The historian Bede tells us that all their buildings

were destroyed, the priests' blood was spilt upon the altars, prelates and people were slain with the sword, and all the cities and churches were burned to the ground. When all was lost and there was no longer a church or home to defend, the Britons retired to the country of their fellow-Christians, the secluded and almost impenetrable hills and forests of the west. The Anglo-Saxon love of gold was quickly recognised by the people of West Wales, who saved their property and bought the right of worshipping after the manner of their fathers by the payment of an annual tribute to their conquerors.

So the British church was swept westward by the Saxon hordes, and the blight of paganism settled once more upon the land. As one would imagine, the conquered Christians would be quite incapable of converting their more virile conquerors, and such conversion as took place at this period would be in the reverse direction, for Christianity was practically dead in this country, until the faith was revived, if not promulgated anew, by other missionaries such as St. Ninian, St. Columba, and St. Patrick.

It has been the fashion of late years to belittle the mission of St. Augustine and to attribute the firm establishment of the Christian church in England, to the above mentioned and other Celtic saints, while some authorities see, in the buildings on Iona, the cradle of northern Christianity, and this

St. Laurence, Bradford-on-Avon.

S. Victor White & Co.

The only Saxon church in England which has not undergone extensive alterations.

Photograph]

A complete Norman Church : Barfreston, Kent.

[Charles S. Harris

Note the wall arcades, and the wheel window with trefoiled lights.

in spite of the fact that the oldest stone of the
existing building is some centuries later in date than
the saint from whom it takes its name.   The Rev.
P. H. Ditchfield puts the case in a nut-shell when
he writes :

> Much learned controversy, many curious arguments,
> have been devoted to the question of the extent to which
> we in England are indebted respectively to the Celtic
> missionaries from the north, the British church in its
> western retreats, and the new mission from Rome under
> St. Augustine.   Each, of course, contributed to the
> evangelisation of Britain.   But that either Celt or Briton
> could have converted the English without the mission
> of St. Augustine is manifestly improbable.   For the
> British church could make nothing of the heathen in-
> vaders before whom it fled.   And the Celts, courageous
> pioneers though they were, lacked the essential gifts for
> consolidating, building up, and organising, those whom
> they converted.   When men began to realise their
> unity, and to look for a centre of life and authority, it
> was to Canterbury and not to Iona that they turned   It
> is unwise and unhistorical to exalt the great work of
> Columba by belittling the great work of Augustine.

At the same time we must remember that Canterbury had become the centre of British Christianity some time before the arrival of the great
Roman bishop.   Bede tells us that there was in the
year 597, in Canterbury, a church " dedicated to
the honour of St. Martin and built while the Romans
still occupied Britain."   When St. Augustine landed
there on our shores one of the first fruits of his
mission was the conversion and baptism of King
Ethelbert, the husband of Queen Bertha.   So we

B

find that although the leaven of Christianity had for long been working in some of the remote places of Britain, possibly for centuries before the Augustinian mission, it was the advent of this great churchman that consolidated the scattered forces of British Christianity, and placed it upon a firm and impregnable basis in line with and under the discipline of the Roman church.   When Augustine and his companions met Ethelbert in the Isle of Thanet, they came " bearing a silver cross for banner, and an image of the Lord the Saviour painted on a board."   In a meadow on the southern shore of the Isle of Thanet stands a stone cross erected some years ago by the late Earl Granville, and placed on the spot, where, according to tradition, St. Augustine stepped ashore, some fourteen miles from Canterbury, the cradle of our English Church.

Chapter II.

Church Plans.*

To the majority of people who are interested in church architecture, and who take a delight in the artistic and romantic appeal made by churches, details concerning the ground plans may seem rather uninteresting. They see there is a porch, a nave, a chancel; perhaps transepts and aisles; and seeing so much they dismiss the question of plan to study with delight some curiously carved capital, or the recumbent effigy of a mediaeval knight.

Yet it must not be forgotten that it is the variety and development of the ground plan that has given us the wealth of variety and detail of the portion of the building we see above the ground, the original small building, large enough at first for the needs of the small population of the parish, having been repaired, enlarged, added to and so on all down through the centuries. In the unravelling of the problems presented by the ground plans often consists the greatest charm of our churches.

The normal plan of our churches is that of two oblong rectangular buildings lying east and west,

* For the evolution of church plans see pp. 149-151.

the western one being the larger and communicating with the smaller by means of an arch-
The Normal Plan. way. The larger building is called the
nave and the smaller the chancel. To.
this normal plan is often added a
square tower west of the nave, and a porch,
generally on the south side. Next an aisle or wing.
north or south, or two aisles, one north and the
other south of the nave are added, and these
communicate with the nave through an arcade, or
series of arches resting upon piers or pillars. A
pillar usually consists of a circular or octagonal
shaft standing upon a base and supporting a
capital, from the top of which the arch starts
or springs. A pier is practically ordinary
walling as though it were, as it often actually
is, the remains of the original wall of the nave
through which the archway has been cut. A
column properly belongs to the classic architecture
of Greece and Italy, and its shaft is either a
monolith (or single stone), or else built up of
drums, each drum being a stone of the full width
and circumference of the shaft. In a pillar, however, the single drums are often replaced by two
stones, one layer with the central joint north and
south ; the layer above with the joint east and
west. A pier is made up of a multiplicity of
stones, and when surrounded, as often, with numerous shafts, is called a clustered pier (48. 65).
Sometimes the chancel also has aisles, or pro-

Homeland　　　　　　　　　　　　　　　　　　　　*Copyright*

Nave of Waltham Abbey Church.

Illustrating a pier arcade, triforium arcade and clerestory. Note the
spiral and zigzag incisions on the massive Norman piers, and vaulting

THE PORCH

North Porch, Arundel Church, Sussex.
A characteristic piece of timber construction.

jecting chapels like aisles. Whether the church has one or more aisles or none, it sometimes has one or two transepts, as they are called, like small chancels built north and south of the nave. So the whole resembles three or four buildings standing at right angles to each other and communicating, by means of arches, with a central space. A central tower sometimes still stands, or once stood, over the crossing (150). Where both transepts occur the plan resembles more or less a cross and such a church is said to be cruciform, though such a form of plan is often the result more of pure accident, and of later additions, than of design. In some Norman churches and much more rarely in later churches, the east end of the chancel terminates in a semicircular or multi-angular extension called the apse (150). Then in later times chantry chapels were often thrown out from nave, or chancel, or transepts The result of all this change and addition due to a variety of causes—fires, earthquakes, repairs, need of enlargement and so on—leads often to very picturesque effects (151)

Although most churches are thus built on a line running east and west, it does not follow that the axes of the nave and chancel are always exactly continuous. In many cases the axis of the chancel is deflected either north or south, to the extent of one or two feet. Many theories have been put forward to account for this deflection without a definite solution being arrived at. It has been stated that the chancel was intended to point to the exact place of the sunrise on the day of the saint to whom the church was dedicated but many churches have been examined with reference to this theory and it has been found that it does not hold good in practice.   A symbolical solution has also been attempted ; that it represents our Lord upon the Cross at that period when His head declined towards His shoulder.

Perhaps all that one is justified in saying is that it is in the churches built or altered during the fourteenth and fifteenth centuries—the great rebuilding period—that these deflections most frequently occur, and that the symbolical interpretation cannot be justified.

We usually enter a church by the porch, which consists of a projection from the main building, although in many instances, as at Cranbrook, Kent, it is formed out of the lower **The Porch.**   story of the church tower.   In early christian days the porch was a place where the uninitiated and the censured could assemble and join in such offices as were allowed to them ; and here also assembled the penitents and catechumens wishing to ask for the prayers of those who entered the church to partake of the communion.   In England down to the Reformation parts of the services for baptism, matrimony, and the churching of women, were here performed. Ancient stoups for holy water may be seen in

or near many porches, but few are to be found
unmutilated.

The large porch or chapel called a " galilee,"
has a history which is largely conjectural. The
finest example is that at Durham Cathedral, which
cathedral is dedicated in honour of the great St.
Cuthbert; and there is an example at Cromer,
Norfolk. These large chapel-like porches were
used on festival and saints' days for the marshall-
ing of the processions before they entered the
church. The term " galilee " has been said to
have been applied to porches situated on the
north side of a conventual church or cathedral,
for the reason that when the crusaders and
pilgrims entered the Holy Land from the north,
Galilee was the frontier province ; but this is more
conjectural than authentic, for J. H. Parker states
that the name was frequently applied to the nave,
or to the western portion of it, as at Leominster,
where a step across the western end of the
nave is called the galilee step. The Durham
Galilee has five aisles and three altars, and the
consistory court is held in it ; that of Lincoln
is at the south-west corner of the south transept, and is cruciform in plan; that of Ely
differs little from an entrance porch. The galilee
of the parish church of Cromer is one of the most
interesting features of a very attractive church.

From the porch we pass into the nave, that
portion of the church situated west of the choir

and chancel, in which the congregation assemble. The word is said to be derived from the Latin *navis*, a ship. The nave usually opens into the

The Nave. tower by a western or tower archway, and into the chancel by an eastern or chancel archway, across which there is sometimes a beautiful screen, or the remains of a screen. If there are aisles the nave opens into these also by archways, so that sometimes the lower part of the nave is an arcade— the nave arcade—on all four sides. The walls north and south supported by the north and south arcades are sometimes pierced by windows looking out over the aisle roofs, so that such a nave is said to be of two stories, the pier arcade below, and the clerestory above. The principal feature in the nave is the font at which the sacrament of baptism is administered. Each section of the church—usually corresponding to each archway on either side below, and each clerestory window above, with the portion of the roof covering that section—is called a bay, so that the nave consists of as many bays as it has archways or windows on each side, except in the case when the entrance doorway takes the place of a window. Normally the nave is of five bays, sometimes more, often less. The entrance doorway is ordinarily in the second bay from the west or four bays from the east or chancel. Besides the font at the west end the nave had normally two altars at the east end on either side of the doorway in the centre of the chancel screen, or, when the nave had aisles, at the east end of the aisles, unless transepts were thrown out for their accommodation.

The word aisle comes from the French *aile*, a wing; hence if a church has a central passage down the nave as well as a passage on either side, we are made to speak of a middle " wing." It is possible that two words have got intermixed, one being *aisle*, a wing, the other *alley*, a place to walk in. Be this as it may **The Aisle.** the north choir aisle of Lincoln Minster was formerly called " Chanter's Alley," and Bishop Pilkington, describing a Whitsuntide service at St. Paul's, said : " In the midst alley their long censer, reaching from the roof to the ground, as though the Holy Ghost came in their censings down in likeness of a dove." In old accounts of our churches the word *alley* occurs as frequently as *aisle*.

Most large churches and many smaller ones have one or two transeptal arms whose axis is at right angles to that of nave and chancel, which extend north and south immediately west-**The Transept.** ward of the chancel. Sometimes, but rarely, these transepts have aisles. Frequently they formed no part of the original design but are later additions Some cathedrals and monastic churches have two sets of transepts.

From the nave we next pass into the chancel—

so named from the Latin word *cancellus*, a screen, from its being screened off. At first rather narrow —sometimes triple—the chancel archway became wider and wider until in later times in some parts of England, as *e.g*, Cornwall, it disappeared altogether, nave and chancel being **The Chancel** one large hall, the chancel being in reality a screened off space, and thus it becomes a ritual and not a constructional chancel. In Herefordshire especially there was frequently no chancel archway even in early churches, and chancel and nave are said to be "telescopic," as though they could be closed up and drawn out at need, like a telescope. As the sacrament of baptism was proper to the nave, the font being placed there, so the mass was proper to the chancel, although as has been said, there were at least two altars in the nave or its aisles or transepts, but the principal mass was said in the chancel, and therefore the altar for this mass—hence called the High Altar—was placed at the east end, the stone font for the sacrament of baptism being at the west end of the nave, and the stone altar for the mass, being placed at the east end of the chancel. Thus these two stone implements for the two great sacraments of Baptism and the Eucharist faced one another, from the extreme ends of the church. Again, as the laity were accommodated in the nave, so also the clergy and those laymen who assisted the clergy were accommodated in the chancel. Normally the chancel consisted of three bays on plan, the western bay or bays containing the stalls for the clergy and their lay assistants, the eastern containing the altar raised on steps, and with usually stone seats—the sedilia—often under beautiful canopy work, on the south side. Near every altar, and near the site of every altar, wherever fixed, there is usually to be found a small recess in the wall containing a stone bowl from which a drain runs down into the earth. This is called a piscina and together with the stone seats, or sedilia, frequently forms part of one design. Wherever we find a piscina we know there was formerly an altar. The subsidiary altars have practically all disappeared, having been removed in consequence of the legislation of 1550. All these things and arrangements are usually shown on the plans of churches, but they will be dealt with more fully in detail in proper order.

When speaking of plans we often include the elevation. The plan, properly speaking, shows the disposition and dimensions of the church, its walls, piers, pillars, etc., as laid out upon the ground, but the elevations show the design and dimensions of the walls with their archways, windows, door-ways, etc., and here it is proper to speak of what **Periods of Architecture.** is popularly, but very misleadingly, known as the periods and the styles of architecture. First there was the manner in which the Saxons planned, designed,

erected, and ornamented and furnished their
churches; then the manner of the Normans,
from *c.* 1050—*c.*1150, one hundred years about,
the work improving and developing as the years
went by, but nevertheless all very conservative;
then two hundred years, *c.* 1150-1350, of the
most beautiful growth and development in the
science of construction and the art of design and
ornament; lastly three hundred years, *c.* 1360-
c. 1660, of settled, fixed, perfect, and conservative
construction and general ornamentation. The
period of growth and development, *c.* 1150-*c.* 1350,
is popularly divided into so-called styles: *c.* 1150-
1190 Transition; *c.* 1175-1245 Early English
Gothic, or Lancet; *c.* 1245-1360 Decorated Gothic
(or *c.* 1245-1280 Early, and *c.* 1280-1315 Late,
Geometrical; *c.* 1315-1360 Flowing or Curvilinear.

It cannot be too strongly pointed out that the
arbitrary divisions into which architectural styles
have been divided—Norman, Gothic, etc.—are
largely imaginary distinctions, as by a series of
easy and almost imperceptible transitions, one
style overlapped and so became merged into the
next, without any hard dividing lines whatever.
These periods during which one style was gradually
transformed into another are called the periods of
transition. When we speak of churches belonging
to the twelfth, thirteenth, or fourteenth centuries,
it must not be supposed that each of these styles

began at the commencement, and died out completely at the end of its century. It may be said
of all living arts, in addition to that of building.
that no style is unaffected by new fashions or old
traditions, or remains stationary for long. Each
style of Gothic architecture grew up slowly, but
continuously, from its incipient to its perfect form,
and then passed gradually into that of its successor.
Always we find there was a putting off of the old
fashion, a putting on of the new, although each
period has left us certain well-defined distinctions
which made each the characteristic style of its
period—grandeur and stability in the Norman ;
stateliness and refinement in the Early English ;
profusion of elaborate detail in the Decorated ; and
vertical lines and fan tracery in the Perpendicular.

For the honour of being our largest parish church
there are three claimants in St. Nicholas, Great
Yarmouth, Holy Trinity, Hull ; and St. Michael,
Coventry (151)   The superficial area of a large
church is, from a variety of causes, a
Large Parish   very difficult thing to arrive at. The
Churches.   available figures, which must be
taken as approximate only, go to
show that the total area in square feet of Holy
Trinity is 25,540 ; that of St. Nicholas 25,023 ;
and St. Michael 23,265. Holy Trinity is some
twenty-five feet longer than St. Michael, and
twenty-four feet narrower than the church at
Great Yarmouth.

The churchyard is commonly regarded as a mere dependency of the church, and as having a history very inferior in interest to that of the temple to which it is the court. The truth is that many of our churchyards are far more ancient than the churches, and some of them may well have constituted the open-air meeting places of our Saxon forefathers long before the erection of parish churches. In this common meeting-place a cross, either portable, or fixed, was set up, around which the worshippers would congregate, mass being celebrated on a small portable altar.

The Churchyard.

The ancient lychgate which forms so picturesque a feature of the few churchyards—about one hundred in number—in which it still remains, takes its name from *lich*, a corpse; so that the lychgate is literally the corpse gate, as Lichfield is the corpse field. Under the shelter of its roof the coffin was rested by the bearers while the opening sentences of the burial service were read or sung by the clergy, who then preceded the procession. Modern lychgates are numerous.

The Lychgate.

Consecration marks indicate where the walls were touched with the holy oil by the bishop when consecrating the building. Ottery St. Mary Church has twenty-one of these crosses, thirteen outside and eight within. These are architecturally treated, each having been set in a quatrefoil, while below several of them the iron supports remain, which on certain great feasts held lights before the con- secration-crosses.

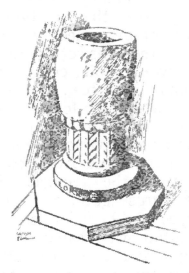

A TUB-SHAPED FONT: SHALDON, DEVON.
(The base is modern.)

Chapter III.

Our Earliest Churches.

THERE are unquestionably many fragments and small portions of pre-Conquest work imbedded in the walls of later churches, and our best ecclesiologists realise that there were as many grades and periods, as many stages of transition, in what is generally called Saxon architecture, as in the more easily followed transitions of the Gothic builders.

Most books dealing with this subject treat only of England and English ecclesiology, omitting all mention of the rest of the United Kingdom. Ireland is especially rich in an architecture of its own, and particularly in buildings and the remains of buildings of the most primitive construction, commencing with beehive huts. These were circular on plan, and built with unmortared stones in circular layers of ever decreasing diameter, until the last smallest circle was crowned by a large flat stone. They were then covered in with earth and sods, larger stones having been left projecting during the course of construction to act as keys or pegs, the better to hold the earth and sods. Afterwards—whether in imitation of the rectangular churches of their Anglo-Saxon neighbours

Saxon work at Barnack, Northants.

(a) Triangular-headed window and pilaster strips, west wall of tower. (b) Doorway, south wall of to
pilaster strips left and over doorway.

Bishopstone Church, Sussex.

A repository of early work: porch is Saxon (long and short work at angles); tower (in four stages marked by set-offs; spire supported by corbel-table) and porch doorway, Norman; windows, Early English.

one cannot tell—the plan changed from circular to rectangular, but the method of construction remained the same till long after the period of the Norman conquest. One of these buildings which remains almost exactly as it was **An Early** when first erected, is the so-called **Oratory.** oratory of Gallerus, in the Dingle, in Ireland ; and if it could be proved that this was erected originally for the purposes of divine worship, one would probably be justified in regarding it as the most ancient Christian church in Western Europe. The form of building resembles a wide-beamed boat turned with the keel upwards. The inside measurement of this " oratory " is 15 feet 3 ins. by 10 feet. The doorway is 5 feet 4 ins. in height, the opposite end having a small window. The masonry, like that of the old clapper bridges on Dartmoor, is held in position without the use of mortar.

A large number of Irish saints made the perilous journey from Ireland to Cornwall, among them St. Piran, who built an oratory **The** on the treacherous sands near Per- **Oratory of** **St. Piran.** ranzabuloe, i.e. *Piran-in-sabulo*. Although the late Max Müller satisfied himself that the word *Piran* meant merely a digger and that St. Piran was a mythical figure, other authorities assure us that the evidence is overwhelming that he was the leader of the band of Irish saints who showed such fondness for the land

c

of Cornwall. The remains of the old church, which, although some two centuries later in date than that attributed to St. Piran himself, may be part of the original church erected in his honour, were excavated and brought to light in the first half of the nineteenth century. The building showed a nave, chancel, and stone altar, and measured externally 29 feet in length, $16\frac{1}{2}$ feet in width, and 19 feet from floor to roof.

St. Martin's Church, Canterbury, has many claims to be considered one of our most interesting churches, no less on account of its associations than

St. Martin, Canterbury. for its structural interest. The date of its building has been a source of endless controversy, as it contains many features attributable either to Roman or Saxon architecture. It is thought that it may possibly have been used for worship by the Christian soldiers of the Roman army. It is probable that on the departure of the Romans the church was still used by a small band of Christian worshippers until the heathen Jutes overran the Isle of Thanet in 449.

As one would naturally expect, the aspect of the structure to-day, though suggestive of antiquity, is lacking in uniformity of treatment. The brick courses in the nave are at irregular intervals, varying from nine to twenty inches apart, the spaces being filled with Kentish ragstone and occasional blocks of chalk. The chancel extends eighteen or twenty feet east of the arch and is composed of Roman bricks, evenly laid and averaging four bricks to a foot. The chancel was lengthened at the beginning of the thirteenth century and again at a more recent date, so that its architecture to-day is of three distinct periods. Outside may be seen five flat pilaster buttresses and one semi-circular one, a square-headed Roman doorway, a Saxon doorway and two Early English porches; and there is also a nearly circular panel on the south side and a Norman squint at the west end of the nave. There are many other features of interest which bear evidences of a great antiquity, and the only question which is seriously disputed is whether the earliest portion of the present nave was built about the end of the Roman occupation of Britain or during the mission of St. Augustine. The Rev. Charles F. Routledge, M.A., F.S.A., Hon. Canon of Canterbury Cathedral, writes : " Whatever may finally be determined to be the date of the church's foundation, it can never lose its unique association with St. Augustine, King Ethelbert and Queen Bertha, nor its undisputed claim to be the oldest existing church in England. From it flowed the tiny spring of English Christianity, which has since widened out into a mighty river, and penetrated the remotest parts of the civilized and uncivilized world."

Among other churches which show signs of having been built during the Roman occupation are those of Reculver, and Lyminge, while the foundations of an undoubted early church have been discovered in the old Roman city of Silchester, in Hampshire. These foundations were uncovered and carefully measured in 1892 (150), and were then covered again for their protection. An exact model, to scale, of the remains can be seen in the museum at Reading.

Other Early Churches.

The old church at Reculver stood originally within the Roman castrum, the fortress which guarded the northern mouth of the Wantsume, now a small stream, but once an arm of the sea dividing the Isle of Thanet from the mainland. The greater part of this church was pulled down in 1809, but the western towers, known as " the sisters," were repaired by Trinity House, as they constitute a useful landmark for mariners, being visible at a great distance.

Reculver Church was built about the year 670, and from the existing walls and foundations it is clear that its plan was basilican. Two stone columns, which supported the triple chancel arch are preserved in the Cathedral Close at Canterbury. An old print showing these columns and arches in the very act of being demolished is reproduced in *Rood Screens and Rood Lofts* (Bond and Camm).

What is, perhaps, the earliest Saxon work now standing, is to be found in the remains of a church near Bradwell-on-Sea, Essex. The building, now used as a barn, formed part of a Saxon church, which most authorities consider to be the actual building there erected in the seventh century by St. Cedd. It stands on the old wall by the Roman city of *Othona*.

Ecclesiologists are now generally agreed that the claim of the church of St. Laurence, at Bradford-on-Avon (16), to be the only Saxon church in England which has not suffered from extensive alterations, is a valid one, although it is doubtful if the existing building is the actual *ecclesiola*, founded by St. Aldhelm, and mentioned by William of Malmesbury. About the year 1857 the late Canon Jones, looking at the roofs of the town from a height, thought he saw the outlines of an old church mixed up with a mass of other buildings. Investigations followed and the church when freed from its surrounding incubus, was found to consist of a nave and chancel, with a porch on the north side and indications of a similar annexe on the south side. The nave measures about 25 feet long by 13 feet broad, the chancel 13 feet long by 10 feet broad ; the porch being about 10 feet square. The height of the nave, and that of the chancel, are both greater than their respective lengths. Two stone figures of angels above the chancel arch bear much resemblance to those figured in the famous Benedictional of St. Ethelwold (A.D. 970-975),

St. Laurence, Bradford-on-Avon.

(British Museum) so that if these figures are coeval with the building in which they are found, we get the approximate date of the present structure, which in that case cannot be the original *ecclesiola* of St. Aldhelm (probably a wooden building) as this famous Bishop of Sherborne died in 709.

About a mile from the town of Bishop Auckland, Durham, is the most interesting and very ancient church of Escomb, which, externally

Escomb Church. bears much resemblance to that at Bradford-on-Avon, though Dr. Hooppell gave its date as the seventh century. Here, too, the building consists of nave, chancel, and porch. The first named measures 43 feet 6 ins. by 14 feet 4 ins., and the great height of the interior is very noticeable. The building after being apparently in constant use for worship until 1863 was, on the erection of a new church, allowed to fall into decay. It was not until 1879 that its interest as a specimen of Saxon work was realised, and its preservation assured.

Brixworth Church (seven miles from Northampton) was, in all probability, founded about 680 A.D.,

Brixworth. by the monks of Medehamstede (Peterborough) to serve both as a missionary and a parish church. Roman materials were used largely in the building, probably taken from the ruins of an old Roman settlement in the district. All the openings are built in Roman bricks. An apsidal presbytery, divided from the nave by a remarkable Saxon arch, is one of the earliest examples. The apse is semi-circular in the interior, but, outside, it forms five sides of a polygon. An ambulatory, round the exterior of the apse, at one time vaulted over, is about six feet below the floor of the church. The western tower is mainly Saxon, probably *temp*. Edgar (959-975 A.D.) A spiral staircase, in a half-round turret, leads to a tower chamber which looks upon the nave and up to the altar through a balustered triple opening.

The church of St. Martin at Wareham, built upon the earlier Saxon ramparts, has some **St. Martin's Church Wareham.** points of similarity with that of Bradford-on-Avon. It possesses similar lofty walls and the inside measurements are much the same. The Wareham church however has been much pulled about and repaired, and its narrow chancel-arch has been fixed as belonging to the early Norman rather than to the pre-Conquest period.

Probably few of our so-called Saxon churches were built earlier than thirty or forty years before the Norman Conquest. Certain it is that pre-Norman buildings in England were singularly rude and rough and show how much our Saxon ancestors were, at that period, behind the Italians, French and Germans in architectural skill.

Our best examples containing Saxon work are

possibly the churches at Sompting, Worth and
Saxon
Churches. Bishopstone (33), Sussex; Bradford-
on-Avon, Wilts (17) ;   Wootton
Wawen, Warwick (sub-structure of
tower) ; Wing, Bucks ; Brixworth,
Barnack (32), and Earl's Barton, Northants ; and
Greensted in Essex. Of towers of this date the
best are possibly those of St. Mary-le-Wigford and
St. Peter-le-Gowt, Lincoln ; St. Peter, Barton-
on-Humber and St. Benet, Cambridge. Of crypts,
the finest examples are at Ripon Cathedral, York
Minster (part), Peterborough Minster and St. Mary
the Younger, York.

Worth is described as " the only cruciform
Saxon church that is in plan complete and un-
touched."   Long-and-short work and pilaster
strips are prominent, and there is a horizontal
string course running round the ap-
Worth.   sidal chancel and the nave. The
nave windows—each with its central
baluster shaft—the typical tall and narrow north
and south doorways— the whole of the former and
the top half of the latter now blocked up—and the
wide and massive chancel arch—probably the
finest Saxon arch now in existence, are interesting
features. The tower is modern.

The tower at Earl's Barton is the most characteristic piece of Saxon work we
Earl's Barton. possess. It consists of four stages,
each slightly smaller than that be-
low it and is highly enriched with pilaster strips.

The characteristic west doorway and the unusual five-fold belfry openings—in Saxon work these are usually double only—divided by baluster shafts, are noteworthy features. The tower arch has been altered in later times.

As at Earl's Barton, the tower at Barnack is elaborately enriched by pilaster strips (32) and it bears much carving. The wide tower arch, **Barnack.** like the chancel arch of Worth, is an exception to the usual tall and narrow Saxon arches. In the interior of the tower in the west wall of the ground storey is a recess possibly originally used as a seat. A feature of this tower is the unusual position of the doorway, viz., on the south side.

Corhampton in the Meon Valley, Hants, presents another example of the Saxon work, and probably differed from the majority of Saxon **Corhampton.** churches in that—like Worth and Brixworth—it possibly possessed an apsidal chancel. Its chief points of interest to-day are the north door arch—now blocked up —the long-and-short work, the chancel arch, the font, and a stone seat in the chancel.

In addition to these mentioned there are many other churches containing Saxon work. Professor Baldwin Brown, in his valuable book *The Arts in Early England*, gives a list of nearly two hundred examples. In a small book of this kind it is obviously impossible to mention every church possessing small or considerable remains of this early period, for possibly every county in England has some fragments to show of pre-Conquest church architecture.

Brief mention, however, may be made of the old church just without the rampart of the famous stone circle of Avebury, Wilts, originally an aisleless building mentioned in Domesday, to **Other** which aisles were added in the twelfth **Pre-Conquest** century. The two round-headed **Remains.** openings in the nave walls are two of the original windows of the Saxon church. They have rebates for shutters flush with the outside faces of the walls and are cut into by the Norman arcade arches which were added to the Saxon church in the twelfth century. In the north clerestory wall there are three circular openings called "wind-holes," two of them cutting into the modern clerestory windows. Mr. C. E. Ponting, the diocesan architect, considers that they belong to the upper tier of Saxon windows which were always open and which gave light when the lower and larger windows were closed.

Although generally consisting of rubble and ashlar, Saxon churches were sometimes built of wood as we see from the existing nave **Greensted** of the parish church of Greensted, **Church,** Essex. A brick chancel has been **Essex.** added at the east and a timber belfry at the west end, but the old Saxon portion is composed of large trees split asunder and set upright close to each other with the round side outwards. The ends are roughly hewn so as to fit into a sill at the bottom, and into a plate at the top, where they are fastened with wooden pins. There are sixteen logs on the south side where are two doorposts, and on the north side twenty-one logs and two spaces now filled with rubble. The body of St. Edmund rested in this church on its translation from London to Bury, in 1013.

It is perhaps worth mentioning here that other churches built wholly or in part of timber are of very much later date. Cheshire is, perhaps, the county richest in these wooden or stave kirks, as the one at Marton, built wholly of wood, and having a graceful timber tower and spire. The aisles are divided from the nave by solid oak pillars, and the south porch roof supported on arches of oak. The other Cheshire examples, such as those of Romiley and Nether Peover (59), are half-timbered buildings, the logs of the latter being filled in with plaster, and those of the former with modern brickwork. Rushton Spencer, in Stafford, has a small half-timbered church, parts of which are said to date back to the time of Henry III, and Essex has a number of timbered towers, of which the finest specimen is perhaps that at Blackmore. The porch here is also of timber.

Chapter IV.

The Norman Church-Builders.

IT has frequently been the custom for the conquerors of a country to write in terms of disparagement about the arts and industries of those on whom they forced their domination, and to regard the conquered races as being little better than savages. This was the Roman and Norman point of view. The British and Saxon has yet to be written, although several writers, amongst them Freeman, speak of the disastrous effect of the Norman Conquest on the native arts and education, an effect which put the English back several hundred years. The Saxon monasteries were great schools of learning, and the Saxon ladies were highly skilled in church needlework and embroidery, their work being known throughout Christian Europe. If the Saxon churches lacked the elements of what we call architecture they were at all events many in number, for the Domesday Survey gives lists of 800 churches existing in four counties only.

The Norman builders appear to have possessed considerable skill in architecture, and many of our English cathedrals still retain some important

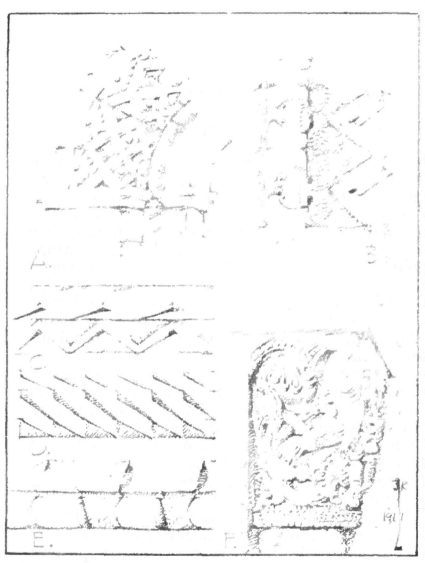

A. Zigzag (enriched): Alsop-en-le-Dale, Derbyshire.   B. Zigzag and

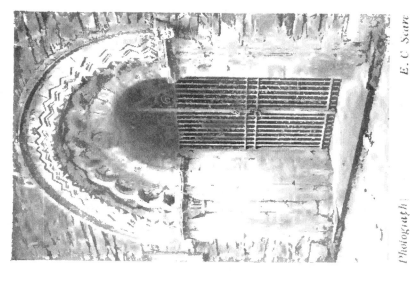

Photograph C. S. Harris

(a) **Barfreston, Kent.**

Observe the carved tympanum, angle-shaft on inner order and nook-shaft in outer order.

ELABORATE NORMAN DOORWAYS

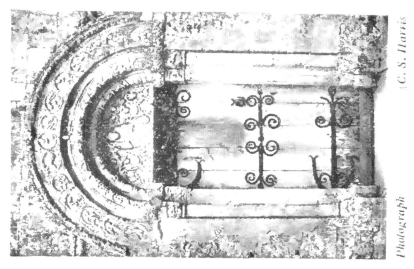

Photograph E. C. Scar

(b) **St. Anthony in Roseland, Cornwall.**

Note the varied forms of the zigzag ornament and multifoiled arch of intermediate order.

Norman work, as for instance the older portions of the cathedrals of Canterbury, Durham, Winchester, Gloucester, Peterborough, Ely, Norwich, Lincoln, St. Albans, Rochester and Oxford.

They were prodigious builders, these Normans, and for a hundred years after their arrival they were building new churches, or rebuilding the old ones which they pulled down for the purpose. The largeness of their architectural conceptions may be seen in the naves of Ely and Gloucester, and particularly in that of Durham Cathedral, among other noble buildings of the period; but massive-looking pillars and walls were often filled in with rubbish, so that their strength was more apparent than real. Their mortar was much inferior to that used by the Saxons. Many of the earlier Norman towers and churches fell from this cause. Hence the great amount of rebuilding in later times. One important fact seems to have escaped all writers on English architecture. The Normans seemed to imagine that all exterior walls must be of solid construction. They therefore made the openings as few and as small as possible, hence where the doorways, which were bound to be larger than mere windows, came, they often strengthened the walls round them, by thickening them. The monotony of these walls with few small openings was in the later and more pretentious building relieved by shallow blind arcading which did not endanger the stability of these mighty walls.

Yet internally they did not fear to poise the immense clerestory walls on piers and arches. At Chichester Cathedral these piers are veritable pieces of walling pierced by archways. When however they came to build the chapel of St. Mary, commonly called St. Joseph's, at Glastonbury, they began to erect actual buttresses. Emboldened by the strength thus gained they flanked the single central window in each bay in the clerestory that had heretofore been the rule, with another window on each side, thus piercing the wall of each bay, with triplets of windows or lights. As buttresses increased in projection, windows (in couplets in the aisles, and triplets in the clerestory) increased in size. At Worcester the triplets in the clerestory are still surrounded by wall, but in the Early English cathedral at Salisbury the wall of masonry, except below and above the windows, has disappeared entirely, giving way to a wall of glass supported by a whole rocky coastline as it were, of promontory and bay, of one continued series of buttresses, jambs and mullions. The sharp edges of the angles of early Norman buildings, of the orders of the arches, and of the jambs and heads of doors and windows, were frequently rounded off and a quirk cut on each face, the result being a bead having the appearance of a pipe let into the exterior angle. In this way arose that beautiful feature of mediaeval architecture—the moulding.*

* See also Appendix D.

The Norman arches were almost exclusively semi-circular. They were sometimes perfectly plain, but larger spans were built in recessed orders which in the early forms were also quite plain edged, as in the pier arcade of St. Albans Cathedral. In later work, however, they were the field for beautiful examples of ornamentation which gradually evolved from rude hatchet work to such intricate and varied examples as those at Barfreston, Kent (45); Tickencote, Rutland (58); Iffley, Oxon., etc.

Norman Arches.

The most general of the later ornaments (44, 58) is the chevron or zig-zag, which is frequently found on arches or windows in two, three or four rows. The next most common form is the beak-head, consisting of a hollow moulding above a large roll-moulding. In the hollow are placed heads of beasts or birds whose tongues or beaks encircle the lower roll. On the western doorway of Iffley Church, Oxon., are many of these beak-heads extending in an unbroken series throughout the whole length of the jambs and round the arch. They also figure prominently among the ornamentations of the church of the Hospital of St. Cross, at Winchester. The less prominent decorations of Norman mouldings include the alternate billet, the double cone, and the lozenge, together with an immense number of others less commonly found.

Norman Ornament.

The massive pillars (54) are distinctive features of the Norman style. The shafts are usually circular, and with capitals, or rather imposts, usually square, but sometimes of the form at Norwich illustrated opposite ; occasionally in plain buildings the pillars themselves are square with very little or no ornamentation. Towards the end of the period, an octagonal pillar was often used, having a much lighter appearance than the earlier forms. Besides these plain pillars, compound or clustered piers are very numerous, differing considerably in plan ; the simplest consists of a square having one or more rectangular recesses at each corner, but one more frequently met with has a small circular shaft in each of the recesses and a larger semi-circular one on each side of the square. The bold decoration of some of the Norman shafts with great spiral and zigzag incisions is notable. A fine example is to be found in the arcades at Waltham Abbey (20).

Norman Piers.

Norman Capitals.

Norman capitals (44, 48) are very varied, having many different forms of ornamentation ; the commonest is one which resembles a bowl, round at the bottom, but with the sides sliced off above, and known as a cushion capital (48), as in the crypt at Winchester. The cushioning is often multi-plied, as at Winchester, and this is then called "scalloping." Sometimes the lower part is cut into round mouldings and is occasionally richly

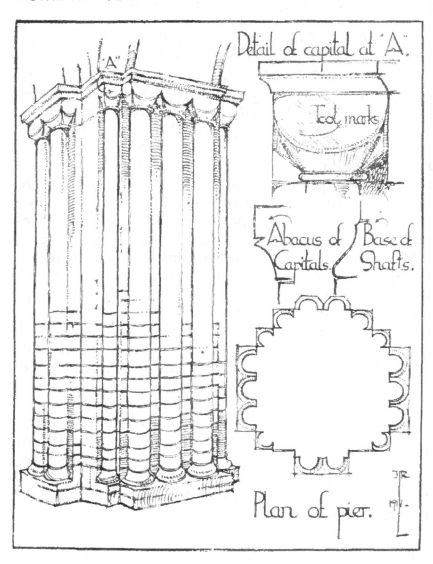

Detail of capital at "A".

Tool marks.

Abacus of Capitals.

Base of Shafts.

Plan of pier.

Taken from the nave of Norwich Cathedral.

A. Iffley, Oxon.   B & C. Tower windows; Icklesham, Sussex.
D. Typical interior of a single light window, deeply splayed.

ornamented, but is frequently left plain. The abacus is nearly always square on plan, flat topped and with a square edge, the under surface being chamfered. The Norman capital in its earliest style was short, but afterwards it became longer, with lighter ornamentation, gradually merging into the Early English.

The earliest Norman windows (49B) were little better than narrow slits deeply splayed on the inside and finished with plain semicir- **Norman Windows.** cular heads, and were generally only a few inches wide. These windows were, it is believed, filled with oiled linen. Later in the period, the stonework round the windows was enriched by the zig-zag and other mouldings and at a still later period an improvement was made by inserting nook-shafts in the jambs similar to those in door-ways. The size of the windows was also largely increased.

The towers of Norman churches often show windows of two lights separated by a central shaft, all enclosed under a large semi-circular arch the spandrel of which is occasionally, though rarely, pierced. Plain circular windows of small dimensions are sometimes found in other positions and occasionally in gable walls. Larger circular windows called "wheel windows," with small shafts radiating from the centre and connected at the circumference by semi-circular or trefoiled arches,

D

are also found, as the fine example at Barfreston Church, Kent (17).

Norman doorways are found in great numbers and variety, even in churches in which all **Norman Doorways.** other traces of this style have been obliterated. The usual form consists of a semi-circular-headed aperture with a hood-mould springing from plain square-edged jambs. Frequently, however, the doorways are recessed, having a nook-shaft in the angle formed by a recession from the capital, in which case the doorway presents two soffits and two faces, besides the hood-moulds. The depth of Norman doorways is largely due to the great thickness of the walls usual in buildings of this period, but in many cases that portion of the wall in which the entrance is inserted was made to project beyond the general face, the projection being finished either with plain horizontal capping, or a high-pitched gable. Norman porches thus have generally but little projection, and are frequently so flat as to be little more than outer mouldings to the inner door. They are, however, often richly ornamented and occasionally project so far as to have a room as an upper storey. The door recess often follows the form of the arch, but the door opening is frequently square-headed, leaving a semi-circular tympanum of masonry filling the space between the lintel of the door and the intrados or soffit of the arch. These tympana are sometimes sculptured in low relief with a representation of some scriptural or traditional event, while the assertion of the Apostle that " we must, through much tribulation, enter into the kingdom of God," may account for the fondness of the Norman sculptors in representing scenes of martyrdom on the tympana of their doors. A noteworthy tympanum is that on the door of the church of Fordington St. George, at Dorchester, whereon is represented an incident in the life of St. George. The principal figure is on horseback with a halo round his head. The other figures generally bear, in point of costume, much resemblance to the figures on the famous Bayeux tapestry.

Barfreston Church, Kent, has an interesting tympanum, (45) as also has Patrixbourne Church in the same county, where the sculpture shows the Saviour with dragons and at his feet a dog. At Alveston Church, Warwickshire, the sculpture shows two quadrupeds with enormous tails, fighting, with between them a small bird, possibly intended for a dove. The best English example of a Norman doorway and tympanum is generally considered to be the west doorway of Rochester Cathedral, where the sculpture is of a very advanced character considering its date, which is probably about 1130-40.

In early Norman work the buttress (53) was almost non-existent, the builders of this period re-

lying for strength upon the great thickness of their walls. It was represented by a broad pilaster slip, with very little pro-
Norman Buttresses. jection, carried from the ground to the corbel table under the roof. Later, however, as the window openings increased in size the projection of these strips was also increased.

A tower is frequently all that remains to us of a Norman church, the remainder having been rebuilt and necessarily enlarged during a later period. It is as a rule remarkable for its massive proportions and the consequent thickness of its walls ; its form is usually square (33, 118). In large churches, there was generally a central tower : in the smaller it is found at the west end but sometimes even in aisleless buildings it occupies a position between the nave and an apsidal sanctuary, as at Newhaven, Sussex. In some flint districts, especially where building stone was difficult to obtain, there are towers circular on plan. In the eastern counties and in Ireland this form is not unusual but it must be remembered that round towers date from pre-Conquest times until the early part of the thirteenth century. Square Norman towers were generally built in three or four stories set off from one another (33). The windows are usually small, round-headed and deeply splayed.

A very good example of a Norman village church may be seen at Studland, Dorset (52).

Photograph   *W. Churchill*

Studland, Dorset; the chancel arch.

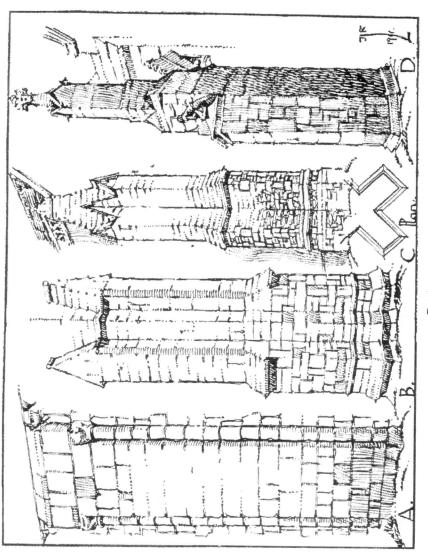

Buttresses.

The building consists of nave and chancel, with a central tower which is very low and stumpy. Under the eaves is a row of corbels grotesquely carved, and others of a not very re-**Studland Church.** fined character may be seen in the nave. The accompanying illustration shows the partial subsidence of the chancel arch, which was found to have been loaded with loose sand. This arch bears the usual Norman mouldings, and some of the nave capitals are vigorously carved with leaves and incised stars. The chancel and the north nave wall have retained their original slits, the other windows having been altered and enlarged. Considered as a whole this early Norman church, although of larger dimensions, does not show a very marked advance on the earlier Saxon churches of Bradford-on-Avon and elsewhere. We know however, that the Norman builders were at work in this country—or the Saxon masons were working in the Norman style—for some years before the Conquest, for Edward the Confessor employed them in building Westminster Abbey, which he commenced in 1050, sixteen years before the Conquest.

The transition from the Norman to the Gothic which followed may be ascribed to the latter half of the twelfth century, when a great change in the construction of the arch began to manifest itself. Alone, however, the form of the arch is no real test of the period. The square abacus, combined with the character of the mouldings, may be taken as the certain mark of Norman work. In its incipient state the pointed arch exhibited a change of form only, whilst the accessories and details remained the same as before ; and although this change gradually led to the Early Pointed style in a pure state, with mouldings and features altogether distinct from those of the Norman, and to the general disuse, in the thirteenth century, of the semi-circular arch, it was for a while so intermixed as, from its first appearance to the close of the twelfth century, to constitute that state of transition called the semi-Norman, which may be seen to very great advantage in the beautiful little Norman church attached to the famous Hospital of St. Cross, near Winchester.

What are known as the round churches, founded by either the Templars or Hospitallers are found at Holy Sepulchre, Cambridge ; Holy Sepulchre, **Round Churches.** Northampton ; (54) St. John, Little Maplestead, Essex ; The Temple Church, London ; Temple Bruer, Lincolnshire. Foundations of a round church have also been discovered at Clerkenwell. The Knights Templars possessed twenty-seven preceptories in England. All these round churches have a direct relation to the Crusades, and they all bear a general resemblance to the Church of the Holy Sepulchre at Jerusalem. The Rev. E. Hermitage Day writes : " Above and around the Holy Sepulchre the

One of the round churches : The Church of the Holy Sepulchre, Northampton.

The cylindrical piers are early Norman work (c. 1100-1108): the pointed arches are a later

VARIETIES OF THE ARCH

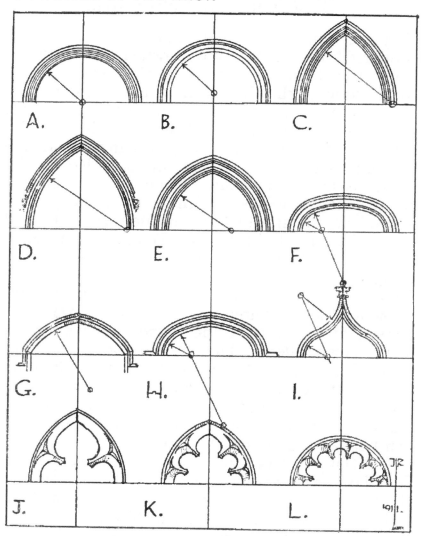

A. Semicircular. B. Stilted. C. Lancet. D. Equilateral. E. Drop Arch.
F. Three-centred. G. Segmental pointed. H. Four-centred. I. Ogee.
J. Trefoil. K. Cinquefoil. L. Multifoil.

Emperor Constantine had built a circular shrine, supported on columns, and crowned with a dome ; while at a little distance from this Anastasis, or Resurrection, the basilican church, called the Martyrium, was erected, connected with the Anastasis by a cloister." Most English examples consisted of a circular building with an inner arcade and an eastern arm, which corresponded to the anastasis and martyrium of the mother church, or to the buildings which were subsequently erected on the site of Constantine's cloister. Of these churches built by the Templars, the least known is that at Temple Balsall, Warwickshire, a village given by Roger de Mowbray, in the reign of Stephen, to the Templars, who built a church and house for their brethren. When the order was suppressed by Edward II the foundation was given to the Hospitallers. The church, not in this case a round church, and old refectory of the knights are still standing. Although the former was restored by Sir Gilbert Scott, in 1849, it is a fine example of a Templars' church, having no division between nave and chancel.

At Temple Grafton, a few miles away, the Templars had another preceptory, but all traces of this building have vanished, as also have those at Temple Combe, Temple Farm, Temple Newsom, etc., where only a name remains to recall their existence. The round churches at Cambridge and Northampton, and the Temple Church, London, are such well known examples that they call for no detailed description.

The preceptory at Little Maplestead was founded by the Hospitallers in 1186. Only the font, however, of the existing church is of that date, the building being a work of the early part of the fourteenth century (some authorities give 1300 as the date of its erection). The church consists of a choir, with an apsidal end, and the nave—formed by the usual round with an inner arcade. To this was added in the fifteenth century a large wooden western porch. The building underwent a drastic restoration about forty years ago, when every window was made new, the arcades scraped, and the porch destroyed. The old altar and rood screen, and the rood stairway, were done away with.

The site of the round church of the Knights Templar at Temple Bruer, has been recently (1909) excavated by Mr. St. John Hope. The round nave is now an open yard with workshops in it, though the tower in three stages is still standing. The excavations were commenced on the site of the rotunda, and disclosed that the diameter of the nave was 27 feet, and that it had eight cylindrical columns in a circular arcade, and an encompassing aisle 9½ feet wide that was lighted by six windows. There was a western doorway to which a porch had been added later, and an arch opened eastwards into the presbytery which had an apsidal termination.

Chapter V.

The Early English Period.

THE origin of what is loosely called Gothic architecture—which is generally considered to include
the styles, with the transitions, from Early English
to late Perpendicular, or Tudor-Gothic—is not
free from obscurity, but the available evidence
goes to prove that the style originated and underwent its earliest developments in the north-west
of Europe, and penetrated by slow degrees to the
south and east. The term Gothic when applied
to architecture, is generally used to denote in one
comprehensive term the ecclesiastical and domestic architecture of the mediaeval period. In
a more confined sense, it comprehends those styles
only in which the pointed arch predominates and
is in that sense used to distinguish them from the
more ancient Romanesque and Norman in which
the semi-circular arch is a leading feature. The
use of the term Gothic in this country appeared
first about the close of the seventeenth century,
and was then used to convey a feeling of contempt
for the buildings so designated.

England was somewhat later than France in
developing this style of architecture, our earliest

complete Gothic being the choir of Wells Cathedral, begun *c.* 1175, although the choirs of Rievaulx and Fountains Abbey were commenced a few years earlier.*   Early English in its earliest developments is nowhere seen to better advantage than in Lincoln and Salisbury cathedrals.

Most of our Gothic buildings were carried out under the supervision of a master-mason, but the most subordinate workman was left plenty of scope within reasonable limits for whatever artistic individuality he possessed, and the enrichments and ornaments of the Gothic era point out the noble aim, the delicate and graceful thought, the refined and exquisite taste expended upon every portion of their buildings by these Gothic masons.

One of the chief differences between pure Gothic and Norman architecture is in the use of the pointed form of arch, yet in the study of the early buildings of this date it is curious to notice how evenly the balance is held between the pointed and the

The Pointed Arch.

* According to most text books, the choir of Lincoln Cathedral, began 1189 or 1190 by Hugh of Wells, is said to be the earliest purely Gothic work we possess, but first it was not so early as the Gothic of Wells or Worcester, and the West generally, and secondly with the later alterations it underwent it looks more purely Gothic now than it originally was, the later thoroughly Gothic additions covering up much of the existing original work, as has been shown only very recently by Mr. Francis Bond, whose discoveries are of the most conclusive character.

Photograph   *H. Walter*

(*a*) Sketch illustrating the origin of window-tracery.

(*b*) **Late Norman Ornament: Chancel Arch, Tickencote, Rutland.**

The mouldings are (from left to right): (*a*) hood mould, continuous fillet
between alternate billets, (*b*) triangular, (*c*) zigzag, (*d*) roll with various

Photograph   A. Bleasdale

Nether Peover Church, Cheshire.

semi-circular arch.   We, looking back, can see
that the Gothic style might have been distinguished either by the semi-circular or the pointed
arch.   In Germany and Italy the former arch
held its own and continued to be used right
through the Middle Ages.   In England, however, the pointed arch soon gained a decided
victory over its rival.   Many theories have been put
forward concerning the introduction of the
pointed arch, one amongst them being that it
was the result of the intersection of two round
arches such as is very commonly found in late
Norman work (64); another theory is the poeti-
cal idea that it was copied from an avenue of trees.
It is quite certain in any case that this form of
arch was known in the East for centuries before it
reached Europe, having been found in cisterns and
tombs in Egypt and Arabia dating from long before
the Christian era.   It has also been suggested that
it was introduced from the east by the Crusaders,
but in that case we should surely have found it
making its first appearance in Hungary, Poland,
Bohemia and Russia, whereas it so happens that
these were the very last countries in Europe to
adopt the pointed arch.   It is, however, now
agreed by the best authorities that the pointed
arch was introduced to meet the exigencies of
vaulting.

The first form of the pointed arch, known as the
Early English, was used from about 1170 (or

even 1150) to 1300 including part of the reign of Henry II, and during those of Richard I, John, Henry III, and Edward I. "Nothing," says the Rev. J. M. Hutchinson, " could be more striking than the change from Norman to Early English. The two styles were the complete opposites of each other, the round arch was replaced by the pointed, often by the acute lancet ; the massive piers by graceful clustered shafts ; the grotesque and rudely-sculptured capitals by foliage of the most exquisite character ; and the heavy cylindrical mouldings by bands of deeply undercut members." But the greatest change of all was the substitution of glass for wall, even such an early building as Salisbury Cathedral being one great expanse of glass.

The Transitional Period.

Gothic architecture differs from all previous forms in the economical use of material, and the small size of the stones used. Whereas in both Roman and Norman buildings the arrangement of the materials depended upon their strength in masses, the Gothic masons employed stones of small size in the construction of their edifices of equal strength and of far greater magnificence ; while in constructive properties the Gothic style was a great advance on anything that had gone before, as the buildings in this style depended for their stability on the correct adjustment of the bearings and thrusts of different arches operating in

A. Three lancets under double dripstone (tooth ornament), the lower following curves of lancet heads, the upper following curve of containing arch: Warmington, Northants. B. Single lancet (interior) splayed: Stanwick, Northants. C. Three lancets: Stanton Harcourt, Oxon.

various directions. Owing to the fact, then, that each portion of a Gothic church helps to support something more than itself, it is obvious that such buildings could be erected with a far smaller quantity of material than was previously necessary. The various little shafts or columns are so disposed as to distribute the weight of the superstructure and thus relieve the greater columns or piers of some portion of the superincumbent weight.

Early English mouldings are very complicated and yet very beautiful, and consist of bead, keel, and scroll patterns, separated by deep hollows giving a rich effect of light and shade round the arch These deeply-cut hollows are also a distinctive mark of the style (60).

The enrichments and little ornaments worked on the mouldings, and particularly those found in the hollows, are most characteristic of the various styles of Gothic architecture. The zig-zag is peculiar to the Norman, the nail-head to the Transitional or semi-Norman, and the **Early English Ornament.** dog-tooth to the Early English. This last ornament represents a flower, looking like four Jordan almonds arranged pyramidically, and there is no other ornament so distinctive of this period (61).

The windows of this period resemble the perfectly plain Norman windows, but with acutely pointed heads, (61) the exterior edge of the jamb being merely chamfered and the interior widely splayed.

Early English Windows. At first used singly they were afterwards placed in pairs along the sides of churches, and in threes and fives or even sevens (1) at the ends. When the window took the form of a two or three-light narrow lancet under one dripstone, the introduction of tracery between the heads of the lancets and the dripstone became desirable for the sake of beauty and lightness of the form, and from the character of its tracery the date of the window can be fairly accurately determined (61). Where the tracery is formed by ornamental apertures pierced through a plate of stone, it is called plate tracery (58, 61), and is generally of not later date than the earlier part of the thirteenth century. If it be bar tracery, with the bars forming plain circles, the work is also Early English, but if, on the other hand, the bars form other shapes, or consist of trefoils or quatrefoils, or other cusped forms, they are of later date. The first approximation to tracery in the heads of windows appears to have been the piercing of the space between the window heads and the dripstone, with a plain lozenge-shaped opening, as at Brownsover Church, Warwickshire.

In the work of this period we find some of the **Early English Doorways.** most charming examples of doorways (64). The deep splay and recessed orders of the Norman opening are retained, and the opportunity thus offered of applying the richly-cut mouldings, delicate shaft-ing, foliaged carving and a wealth of the pre-vailing tooth ornament, was taken to its fullest extent. The large doorways were frequently double.

Early English porches project much further from the main walls to which they are at-

Early English Porches. tached than do the Norman as a rule, and in large and important buildings they occasionally have a room above.

The gables are usually bold and high-pitched, and the interiors, as at Wells, Ely, etc., quite as rich in design as are the exteriors.

Gothic capitals are either moulded (or without foliage) or foliaged. Early English moulded capitals are usually of the shape of an inverted bell, and are, in the smaller examples, quite devoid of ornament, with the exception of a necking and one or two mouldings

Early English Capitals, and Piers. round the abacus. The bell is gen-erally deeply undercut and this un-dercutting, as in the mouldings, is an Early English characteristic.

The nail-head and dog-tooth ornaments sometimes appear in the hollows between the mouldings. In the large examples the bell is covered with foliage, which springs direct from the lower ring of the capital, called the necking or astragal (60, 65). The stalks are generally grouped together and curl over most gracefully beneath the abacus. In clustered piers (65) the capital follows the form of the pier (which in England falls into one of three classes : the Western with attached shafts in groups of three, the Southern with detached shafts and the Northern, the ordinary clustered pier. The Western lasted only from *c.* 1170—*c.* 1200 and the Southern from *c.* 1170— *c.* 1300,) and they also adopt the same form in the single shaft, with the exception that multi-angular shafts have often circular capitals. The base consists of a series of mouldings and frequently stands upon a double or single plinth, which in the earlier examples is square, but in later examples assumes the form of the base, and is either circular or polygonal. In Stone Church, near Dartford, Kent, is a good example of an Early English capital, decorated with stiff-leaved foliage, and the dog-tooth ornament, which in this case is also between the mouldings of the arch. In small churches a plain octagonal or circular pier is most frequently used ; and as this form of pier was used largely in the Decorated or succeeding style it can only be distinguished by its mouldings and ornaments.

The buttresses of this period are, as a rule, simple in form, and in small churches consist of two or more stages, each set-off or division being sloped at the top to carry off

Early English Buttresses. the rain. A characteristic of early buttresses is their disposition at the angles of churches—they were always set in pairs at right angles to each other (53). Later

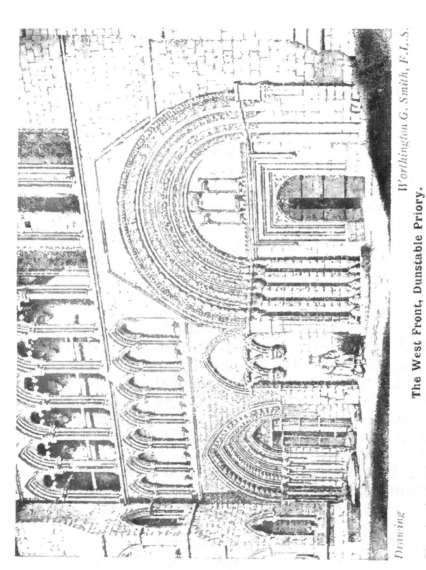

Drawing

Worthington G. Smith, F.L.S.

The West Front, Dunstable Priory.

Showing late Norman and Early English work side by side, and intersecting round arches (see page 50), together with remnants of book-shafts in doorways. Note also dripstone label over square headed inner doorway.

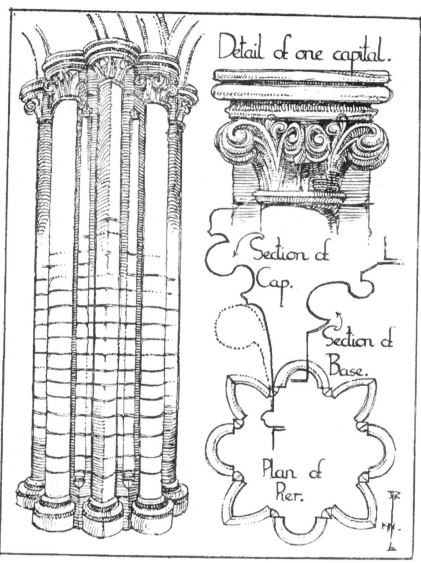

Detail of one capital.

Section of Cap.

Section of Base.

Plan of Pier.

Rye, Sussex.

ones were set singly and diagonally (1).   In
larger buildings the buttress generally finishes
with a gabled head, and is frequently carried above
the parapet, except where stone vaulting is used,
in which case it is covered with a pinnacle either
plain or ornamented.   The edges are often chamfered or the angles ornamented with slender shafts.
A niche to contain a statue is occasionally sunk
in the face of the buttress, but this feature is
more common in the next or Decorated period,
although the change from one period to another
was so gradual that the exact date of a niched
buttress would be difficult to determine were
there no other features to guide us.

External flying buttresses were first introduced
at this period, and are common in all large buildings with vaulted ceilings. They are generally
of simple design, with a plain capping and
archivolt, and they spring from the top of the
wall-buttress and abut against the clerestory to
receive the thrust of the main vault. (82).

The most ornate examples of Gothic architecture may be said to have been erected between
the years 1180 and 1300, and from the latter
year many writers date the commencement of
its decline.   In England we owe nearly the
whole of such magnificent buildings as the
cathedrals of Lincoln, Salisbury, Worcester, and
the abbey church of Westminster to the thirteenth
century, and there is scarcely a cathedral or

E

abbey that does not owe some beautiful portion of its structure to the builders of the same period, the north transept and lady chapel of Hereford Cathedral, the eastern transepts of Durham, the nave and transepts of Wells, the transepts of York, the choir, presbytery, central and eastern transepts of Rochester, the eastern portion of the choir of Ely, the west front of Peterborough, the choir of Southwell, the nave and transepts of Lichfield, and the choir of St. David's being a few of our most characteristic examples of this period.

Interior Elevation   A.

Plan of Window   D

B.

C.

A. Winchelsea. Sussex (an unusual example : note blind arch at each

Photograph   *W. E. Fitzgerald*

St. John's Hospital Chapel, Northampton.

The window is an excellent specimen of intersecting and curvilinear
tracery. The photograph also shows a modern rood-beam bearing the

Chapter VI.

The Decorated Period.

THE period which followed the Early English is known as the Decorated, the Geometric form of which embraces roughly the second half of the thirteenth century (see pp. 10 and 28) and the opening years of the fourteenth century, while in its later or Curvilinear form the Decorated continued until the ravages of the Black Death in 1349-50.

In England the most perfect examples are perhaps not to be looked for in cathedrals and large churches, but in their chapels. The most superb specimen we possessed, St. Stephen's, Westminster, was partly destroyed by the fire of 1834, and of the two chapels only the lower one now remains. Those left to us include the chapel of the palace of the Bishops of Ely, in Ely Place, Holborn, now the Roman Catholic church of St. Etheldreda, as representing the Geometrical form; and Holy Trinity Church, Ely, once the Lady Chapel, and Prior Crawden's Chapel, near by, as representing the latest development of the Curvilinear, while the former is considered the most highly-wrought building in England. Belonging to this period, also, is the choir of Merton College Chapel, Oxford, and the nave of Exeter.

The Decorated work, as has been said, may be divided as regards its windows into the two classes—Geometric and Curvilinear, and it is from the tracery of the windows that these names are derived.   The former has tracery evolved entirely from the circle.   The latter **Decorated** is distinguished by traceries formed **Windows.** by ogees or flowing lines.   (66 C).

Decorated windows (66) are usually large and contain from two to seven lights, although there are many windows with a single light, but of less elongated form than those of the Early English period.

As we have seen in a previous chapter, tracery originated from the desirability of piercing that portion of the wall which was left vacant when two lights were gathered under a single arched dripstone, and therefore elementary tracery consisted merely of apertures in a flat surface.   As by the introduction of the buttress the necessity for large expanses of wall ceased, the desire for light and the warmth of the sun's rays led to the enlargement of the windows, but as leaded glass needs support, mullions and tracery were necessarily multiplied.   The Geometric tracery, as we have seen, consists of various combinations of the circle, as the trefoil, the quatrefoil, the cinquefoil, etc.

In Curvilinear windows the tracery, although

Lady Chapel, St. Alban's Cathedral, c. 1295-1326.

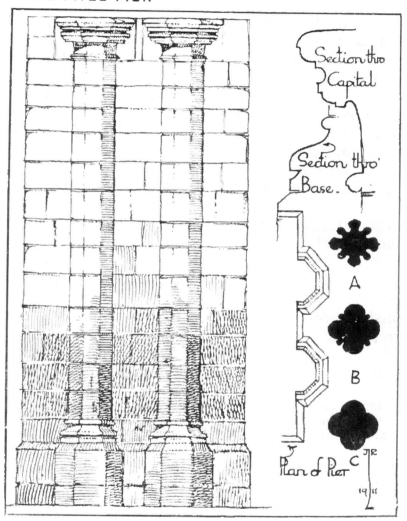

Section thro Capital

Section thro' Base.

A

B

Plan of Pier C

A typical example of a pier of the Decorated period.

A B and C. Plans of characteristic Decorated piers. These illustrate the gradual disappearance of the pear-shaped hollows and projections, and the increasing simplification of plan.

based on the same forms and figures, is yet so blended into an intricate pattern that each figure does not stand out with the same individuality as in the Geometric (70).

Among our most beautiful Geometric windows are those of the Lady Chapel at Exeter, and Merton College Chapel, Oxford, and of the Curvilinear our best example is probably the east window of Carlisle Cathedral.

It must be noted that beautiful as is Curvilinear tracery, yet it marks a certain decadence in Gothic architecture, in that it is an irrational treatment of stone, and conveys the idea that the material was bent and not cut into the required shape (70), it being a well-established canon of criticism that a decline in art is marked when constructional requirements are sacrificed to pure ornament.

In plan Decorated capitals follow that of the column, cluster or pier, and are usually of a bell-like form. They are frequently only **Decorated Capitals and Piers.** moulded, thus presenting rounds, ogees, and hollows, on which the prevailing ornaments of the period, the ball flower and the square flower, are set. The foliaged sculpture is most exquisite, and is gracefully wreathed around the bell, instead of rising from the astragal of the capital, as in the earlier style (71 A). Many varieties of leaf and flower are represented the oak, the vine and the rose

being perhaps the most common, but the leaves
of the maple, hazel, ivy and strawberry are all
so beautifully rendered as to evidence their having
been directly studied from nature.   Plucked
flowers are frequently represented, and sometimes the little stalks and foliage are interwoven
among birds, lizards, squirrels and other animals.
The piers of this date are much more elaborate
than those of the Early English style, and in
Decorated plan have curved outlines with
Ornaments. moulded members between the
shafts (69). The mouldings (71) are
very varied, but the hollows not
being so deeply undercut, the general effect is
broader and less liney than in the Early
English (60) ; while the Decorated arches are
less sharply pointed.

The doorways of this style possess much the
same features as the last, but the mouldings, jamb
Decorated shafts, etc., are more slender, and
Doorways. the hollows are often filled with the
ball-flower and square flower instead
of the dog-tooth (71).   Sometimes
the doorways have no shafts, the sides or jambs
being entirely composed of mouldings which are
continuous with those in the arch above.   The
large single doorways of this period are nearly as
large as the double ones of Early English date,
and on the sides small buttresses or niches are
sometimes placed, and frequently a series of

Photograph   Gardner

East Sutton, Kent.

DECORATED ORNAMENT

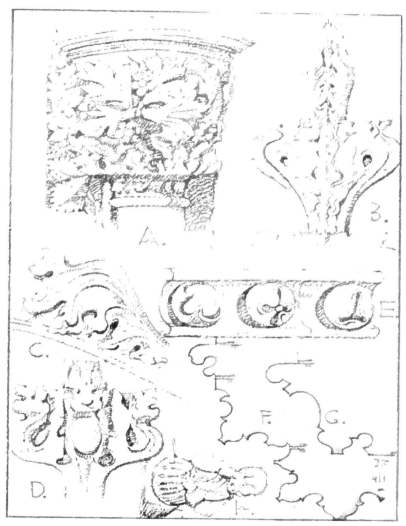

A. Capital: Southwell. B. Finial: Lavenham, Suffolk; C. Crocket:
York. D. Crocket: Canterbury. E. Types of ball-flower enrichment.
F. Section of arch-mould: St. Mary, Beverley. G. Section of arch-
mould: Glastonbury. H. Gargoyle at Merton College, Oxford.

niches carried up in a hollow moulding and filled with figures will be found.

The buttresses in the Decorated are nearly always worked in stages, and a niche frequently figures on the face of the buttress. **Decorated Buttresses.** Crocketed canopies and other carved decorations are common in large buildings and the buttresses usually terminate in pinnacles, which are sometimes of open work (53).

The nave of Exeter Cathedral is possibly the best example of Decorated building on a large scale we possess, the variety of its window tracery being especially noteworthy.

AN ANCIENT CHEST.

Chapter VII.

The Perpendicular Period.

ALTHOUGH the choir and transepts of Gloucester Cathedral had been changed from heavy Norman to skeleton construction as early as 1331-1377, it was not until towards the close of that century, that this great change in Gothic architecture became general. The Curvilinear tracery gradually gave place to a rigid vertical and horizontal form, with the result that window-heads and panels instead of being filled with curved bars of stone, were sub-divided by straight perpendicular bars and transoms or cross-bars. This style of tracery is popularly known as Perpendicular, although a more rational name for it is that adopted by Mr. Sharpe, viz. Rectilinear, This change in form of the tracery made its appearance during the fourteenth century, although it was by no means wholly introduced at that period, for the old methods and styles were carried on side by side with the new for many years. For example, the eastern end of the choir of York Minster (1361-99) possesses a window the traceries of which contain both curvilinear and rectilinear lines, while Shottesbrook Church in

Berkshire (1387), and Winnington Church, Bedfordshire (1391) are examples of village churches neither of which has any feature of the Perpendicular.

There are more churches of this character, and they are as a rule larger, owing to the fact that as this period lasted from c. 1360 to 1660 or three centuries, while Norman and Transitional and Early English and Decorated were all crowded into but two centuries, first, there was naturally more building and rebuilding in this period ; secondly, the population of each parish was much greater than in the earlier times ; and lastly, no other distinctive style followed this to alter and upset the plans of the fine large churches built or entirely rebuilt in later times when the population was greater, much wealthier, and enjoying peace such as was impossible under the continued state of war at home or abroad from the Conquest till the marriage of Henry VII. The plans of churches in this style differ from all others in that they are more   spacious, and more regular.   The columns are also more slender and farther apart, the windows much larger, the walls loftier and thinner, and the piers occasionally panelled (81).

In its earlier stages the Perpendicular presented an effect at once good and bold ; the mouldings, though not equal to the best of the Decorated style, were well defined, the enrichments effective, and the details delicate without extravagant minuteness. The flowing contours and curved lines of the previous period now gave place in the windows to mullions running straight up to the enclosing arch, and crossed by transoms. In early buildings of this period the drop-arch, common at all times, is very prevalent, but as the period advanced a form known as the Tudor arch began to be used (55). It is one which, as a rule, consists of arcs of four circles, struck from centres of which those of the two upper or inner arcs lie immediately below those of the two lower or outer arcs; but this is not always the case for sometimes the whole of the upper portion uniting the two outer arcs is the arc of a single circle struck from a centre between and below the centres of the circles of which the outer arcs form portions. Towards the close of the period the curvature of the upper portion of the arch is sometimes so slight that it can hardly be distinguished from a straight line, and as the debasement progressed it became really straight. Ogee arches (55) are also found at this period (as in the Decorated), and foiled arches are very frequent.

The peculiar characteristics of the windows—the vertical mullions carried right up into the heads (75, 82) and the horizontal transoms—we have already alluded to. The window heads, instead of being filled with flowing tracery, have slender mullions running from the heads of

Perpendicular Windows.

Magdalen College, Oxford.

A typical Perpendicular doorway.

The Eleanor Cross, Northampton.

A beautiful example of Decorated work.

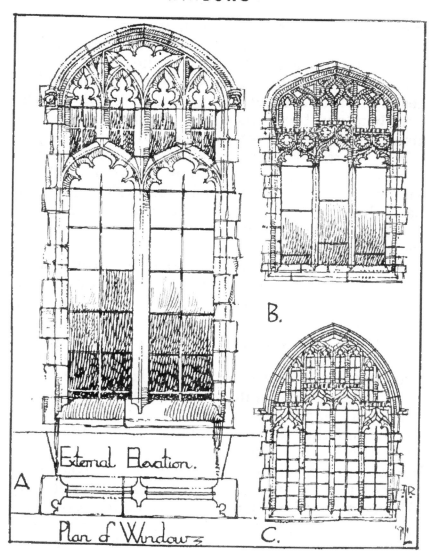

A. Melbourn, Cambs.   B. St. Andrew, Norwich.   C. Playden, Sussex.

the lights between each main mullion, and these again have smaller transoms, until the whole surface of the window-head and often of the whole window becomes divided into a series of panels, the arched heads of which are trefoiled or cinque-foiled.   In the later windows the transoms at the top are often furnished with a small ornamental battlement (75).

The Perpendicular builders not infrequently filled up plain openings such as Norman windows, with their tracery, as we may see in Peterborough Cathedral and Tewkesbury Abbey, where great Norman windows are so filled; so also they filled the lancets at Wells.

The doorways of the early portion of this period had two-centred arches, but the characteristic form is the four-centred, enclosed in a **Perpendicular** square head, formed by the outer **Doorways.** mouldings with a hood mould of the same shape, the spandrels being filled with quatrefoils, roses, shields, etc. (74, 82).

Perpendicular capitals are either circular or octagonal, but the necking is usually of the former shape, and the upper members of the abacus of the latter form.   The bell portion is mostly plain, but is often enriched with foliage of a conventional character, shallow and formal, characterised by vigour and good craftsmanship, though not possessing either the freedom or the boldness of the Early English, or the exquisite grace of the Decorated periods (76).

The mouldings of this period are essentially different from those which preceded them. As a general rule they are cut on a slanting or chamfer plane, the groups of mouldings being separated by a shallow oval-shaped hollow, entirely different from those of the Decorated period (76 F).

A very characteristic ornament is the Tudor flower (76 A). It is formed by a series of flat leaves placed upright upon their stalks. **Perpendicular ornament.** It was much used in late buildings as a crest (76 E) or ornamental finishing to cornices, etc., to which it gave an embattled appearance. Cornices and brackets were frequently ornamented with busts of winged angels and were in that case called angel-brackets, and angel-corbels. The portcullis and the Tudor rose—both badges of the house of Tudor—also figure prominently among the ornaments of the period. The crockets for the most part partake of the squareness which pervades all the foliage of this style (76 D).

The buttresses in their plainer forms, are very similar to those preceding them, but in richer examples the faces are covered with **Perpendicular buttresses.** panel work and are finished with square pinnacles sometimes set diagonally and terminated with a crocketed spire, or finished with the representation of an animal, or other ornament (53). Parapets with square battlements are very common

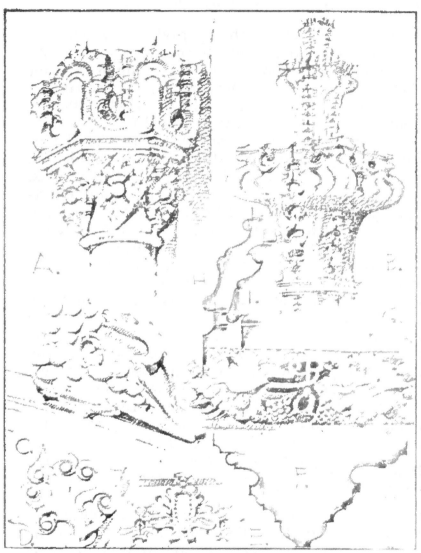

A. Capital: Lavenham, Suffolk.   B. Finial: Canterbury.   C. Crocket.

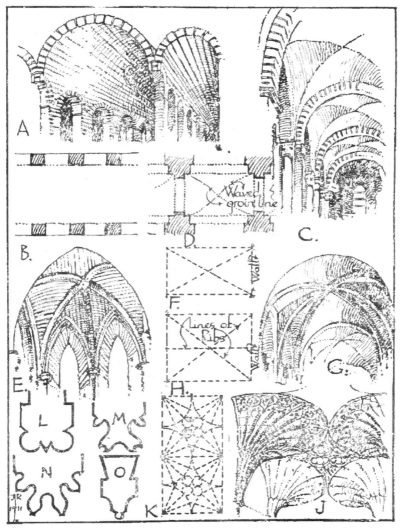

A & B. Barrel vault with plan. C & D. Groined vault with plan.
E & F.—G & H. Ribbed vaults with plans. J & K. Fan vault with
plan. L. Norman vaulting rib. M. Early English vaulting rib.
N. Decorated vaulting rib. O. Perpendicular vaulting rib.

at this period, but they too are frequently either panelled, or pierced with tracery or with trefoils or quatrefoils inserted in square, circular or triangular compartments.

Panelling (82, 83) is occasionally used abundantly on walls, both internally and externally, and also on vaulting, while some buildings, as the incomparable Henry VII's Chapel at Westminster, are almost entirely covered with it.

English vaulting had always been a thing of itself. From the simple arrangement of two diagonal ribs crossing each other midway between the transverse ribs separating each severy of the vault, gradually the number of ribs increased and multiplied, first single intermediate ribs and ridge ribs were added, then the intermediate ribs were continued as lierne or cross ribs and still more intermediate ribs until finally the fan vaulting so characteristic of this period was reached (77). In the earlier vaulting all the ribs reaching to the ridge of the vault necessarily varied in length, but in fan vaulting they were made of the same length and curvature, and hence left a space in the centre of each severy of the vault without ribs. This was filled with panelling or with a complete pendant cone, whereas the fan formed by the ribs was either a semi-cone or quarter-cone more or less. As English Gothic began in the West, as Perpendicular began in the West, so the earliest examples of fan vaulting occur at Tewkesbury and Gloucester in the West.

The roofs (80) of this period, both in ecclesi-astical and secular buildings, are very magnificent, and have the whole of the framing ex-**Perpendicular** posed to view ; many of them are of **roofs.** high pitch, the spaces between the timbers being filled with tracery, and the beams arched, moulded and ornamented in various ways ; and frequently pendants, figures of angels, and other carvings are introduced. The flatter roofs are sometimes lined with boards and divided into panels by ribs, or have the timbers open, and all enriched with mouldings and carvings, as at Cirencester Church, Gloucestershire. The hammer beam roof in the church of Wear Gifford, Devon, is possibly the finest example of its class in the county, while other notable roofs are those at St. Peter's, St. Andrew's and St. Mary's, Norwich ; Knapton, and Trunch, Norfolk ; those at Harrow and Ruislip, Middlesex ; Long Melford and Southwold, Suffolk ; Saffron Walden and Thaxted, Essex, and a particularly fine one at St. David's Cathedral in Wales. Among the remarkable domestic roofs in this style are those at Westminster Hall and Eltham Palace.

The chief characteristics, then, of the Perpendicu-lar style are the two main mullions carried right up to the heads of the windows, the transoms, and the general flattening of arches, mouldings and carv-ings. Should there be no other guide, a Perpen-dicular church carries its style and period stamped upon its carvings. The plants represented are, almost without exception, the vine with or without grapes, and the oak with or without acorns. The leaves are generally full grown and crumpled. The Perpendicular style is seen to advantage in the beautiful little priory church of Edington, in Wilts, erected by William Edington, Bishop of Winchester. The same style, but more fully developed, is seen in the nave of Winchester Cathedral, at New College, Oxford, and at Winchester College. We must, however, bear in mind that the solidity of the Winchester nave as a whole is due almost entirely to the original Norman work of Bishop Walkelin, which the Perpendicular merely encases.

Bishop Wykeham, at once prime minister, diplomatist, scholar and energetic churchman, will always be remembered by posterity as one of the most remarkable geniuses of the middle ages, a man of giant mind and immense physical energy, who impressed upon all his work the unmistakable personality of a master.

His architectural work, as is to be seen at St. Mary's College, Winchester, and the other " St. Maries College at Oxenford," commonly called New College, marks a very decided epoch in our national architecture. His buildings appear at first sight to be so simple as to suggest that their designer cared more for the constructional than the artistic side of building, although what

little ornament is used is studiously careful and
effective.　It is the freedom from masses of highly
wrought ornament which made his early Perpendicular buildings such a contrast to the
exuberance of the previous period, or the over
elaboration of the Tudor work that followed it.

Perpendicular architecture is essentially English,
which is the more remarkable considering that
up to this time there had been strong points
of resemblance in the Gothic art of all the northern nations　While the Perpendicular is essentially the English Gothic, French Gothic tracery
developed into the flamboyant.*

This Flamboyant is the intermediate form between the French Decorated of the fourteenth,
and the Renaissance style of the sixteenth century,
and is contemporary with our Perpendicular work.
With the exceptions of some wooden screens and
stall-work in the North of England, as in the
churches of Hexham and Jarrow, and in some of
the carved wooden chests retained in our churches
(all of which are apparently of foreign workmanship),
and of an occasional instance such as the windows
of the Monastery at Rye, the style found little or
no favour in England, although something ap-
proaching it may be seen in Scotland, where
French builders were frequently employed, in the

*So called from its *flame*-like appearance, producing forms
which resemble elongated tongues of flame.　The finest
example is Chartres Cathedral.

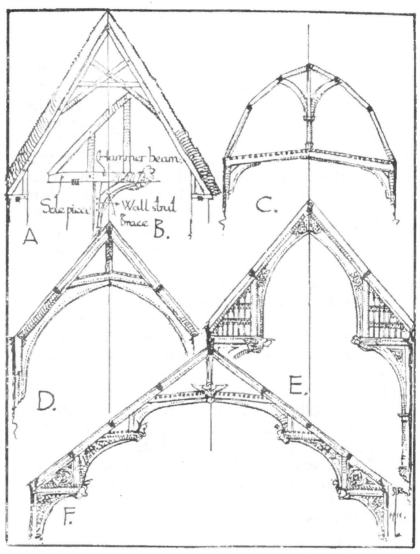

A. Trussed rafter.   B. Diagram illustrating the hammer beam.   C. King post waggon roof.   D. Collar brace roof.   E. Single hammer beam roof. F. Double hammer beam roof

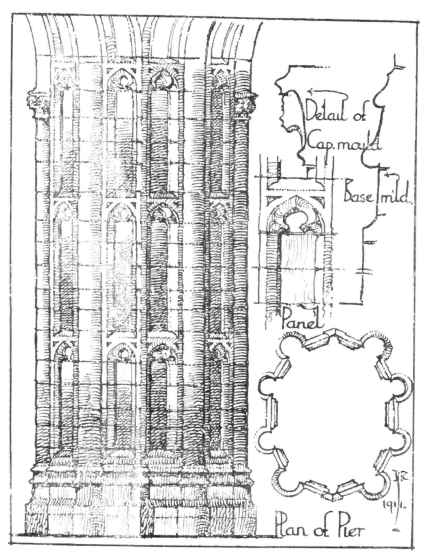

Detail of Cap. mould

Base mould.

Panel

Plan of Pier

Sherborne, Dorset.

days when Scotland and France were temporarily united in arms against England.

As builders and designers of church towers the masons of the Perpendicular era have never been approached, and all our finest English towers are of this style and period (118). Considerations of space will only allow a few of these towers to be mentioned, but among the finest are those at Boston, Lincolnshire (118) : Wrexham, Denbighshire ; Wymondham and Heigham in Norfolk; Southwold Church in Suffolk; St. Mary Magdalene, Taunton (118) ; and Manchester and Newcastle Cathedrals : the tower of the last named having flying buttresses that spring from corner turrets and support an elegant lantern. Of Perpendicular date and style, also, are the great lantern towers of Worcester, Bristol, Gloucester, York and Durham Cathedrals, and the fine bell-tower of Evesham Abbey.

Perpendicular towers.

If, considered as a whole, East Anglia is the land of roofs, and Devonshire that of rood-screens, Somerset is the home of towers, though the architectural genius that filled this shire with towers also flowed into Wales. Wiltshire has a few delightful towers, and Dorset has in Beaminster one so rich in design and sculpture that it has no equal in this county which, however, has a fine Perpendicular church at Milton Abbas, Dorset, a building that takes high rank in its class.

F

Although nearly all our cathedrals have some portion of their fabric in the Perpendicular style, chantry chapels, cloisters, vaulting, screens, etc., it was in our parochial churches that Perpendicular architecture reached its highest and finest development.   Just as the thirteenth century was the great age for cathedral building, so the latter end of the fourteenth and the earlier half of the fifteenth centuries was the period to which we owe some of the most beautiful of our parish churches, as St. Michael, Coventry (finished 1395); St. Nicholas, Lynn (fin. 1400) ; Manchester Cathedral (formerly a collegiate church), 1422 ; Fotheringhay Church, Northants (fin. 1435); Southwold Church, Suffolk (1440), and St. Mary Redcliffe, Bristol (about 1442).   A little later came, among others, Wakefield, Yorkshire (1470), St. Stephen's, Bristol (1470), St. Mary, Oxford, and its namesake at Cambridge (both in 1478) and Long Melford Church, Suffolk (1481).   Lincolnshire has a fine group of Perpendicular churches, and another good set may be found in the Cotswolds at Chipping Campden, Winchcombe, Northleach, Cirencester, and Fairford.

Terrington St. Clement, Norfolk.

Henry VII Chapel, Westminster Abbey.
A corner of the chapel which is perhaps
the most glorious example of Perpendicular work in England.

Chapter VIII.

The Renaissance and After.

BEFORE we turn our attention to the change in church architecture which, speaking generally, followed the Perpendicular, it is necessary to define what elements entitle a building to the name Renaissance, and when and where we find the various ingredients of the style combined. Many authorities consider that the term Renaissance is too loosely applied, and should be restricted to work which unites both the Gothic and Classical elements—a combination in which Gothic forms and principles are modified and partly replaced by something classic. It has been fittingly said that the art of the Renaissance contains three souls—the soul of classical antiquity, the soul of Christianity, and the soul of the Northern races ; and that no one of these impulses can be disregarded in a study of the Renaissance, its origin, characteristics, and development.

This Renaissance or re-birth of classic art did not at once displace the older indigenous forms, and the old features remained for many years side by side with the new, with the result that until the masons succeeded in freeing the new styles of classical architecture from the Gothic element, they produced an extraordinary blend of the two styles. At first the new style had but small influence on the English craftsmen of the time, and until the end of the sixteenth century the Gothic tradition lingered on in this country where for many years the Renaissance style was used only for tombs, screens, and the minor details of large churches. Mr. Fergusson, in his *Modern Styles of Architecture* says "Our Gothic buildings being evolved by the simple exercise of man's reason show instinctively the natural growth of man's mind, whereas those buildings designed in the imitative styles more often than not degrade architecture from its high position, of a quasi-natural production to that of a mere imitative art." Gothic enthusiasts go so far as to say that no perfectly truthful architectural building has been erected in Europe since the Reformation. At the same time we must remember that Gothic architecture had reached, so far as we know, its utmost limits of development, and the attempt to revive the Gothic style in the nineteenth century after a series of trials extending over sixty years, was, with a few exceptions, a complete failure. After the Renaissance had succeeded in shedding all traces of the Gothic influence it became the fashionable style for both secular and religious buildings.

The first really able exponent of Renaissance

architecture in England was Inigo Jones, whom
James I, appointed surveyor-general of the works,
and who in the succeeding reign had charge of the
rebuilding of old St. Paul's Cathedral. The
traditions and ideas introduced by Inigo Jones,
were continued by Sir Christopher Wren when
the work of wholly rebuilding that cathedral
became necessary after its destruction in the
Great Fire of 1666.

Our most remarkable church in this style is St.
Paul's Cathedral. It bears so great a similarity
to the great church of St. Peter, at Rome, that one
cannot help comparing it with that fine example,
and it is the only English Protestant cathedral
which is not in the Gothic style. If, as some
critics claim, St. Paul's falls short of St. Peter's,
especially in its lighting, it does not deserve
the condemnation of a great German critic, who
said, " It is a building marked neither by elegance
of form nor vigour of style." Although the interior of its dome and clerestory of the nave and
choir are extremely gloomy when compared with
those of St. Peter's, the church is generally acknowledged to be far superior to the latter in its architectural details, and few, if any, Italian churches
can be said to surpass it, either in general composition or external effect.

Other churches which are excellent examples
of this style are St. Stephen's, Walbrook, and St.
Mary Abchurch, London. Both show remarkable

skill in design.   The first-named is divided into a nave and aisles, transepts, and a shallow chancel, by four rows of Corinthian columns, with a small dome over the intersection (87).   The interior is very beautiful, and this church is generally considered to be Wren's masterpiece. St. Mary Abchurch is nearly square on plan, has no columns and is covered with a domical ceiling, but is so skilfully treated that the effect is singularly pleasing.   Here it may be said that the interior of many of Wren's churches owe much for their enrichment to the wood-carving of Grinling Gibbons.   The churches of St. Mary le Bow, Cheapside; St. Bride, Fleet Street; St. Mary le Strand (86) and St. Magnus the Martyr, Lower Thames Street; have noteworthy examples of Wren's steeples.

The style which we now call Queen Anne came in towards the close of the seventeenth century, and belongs of right to the reign of Charles II.   Hawksmoor was **Hawksmoor.** a strong architect who has left us Christ Church, Spitalfields, St. George's Bloomsbury, and St. Mary Woolnoth. He also completed the western towers of Westminster Abbey, designed and commenced by Wren, and he designed the second quadrangle of All Souls' College, Oxford.   This architect, like the majority of his contemporaries, misunderstood and despised the Gothic work, with

An eighteenth century
steeple by James Gibbs.
St. Mary-le-Strand, London.

St. Stephen, Walbrook, London.

excellent example of Renaissance architecture: generally accepted as the masterpiece of Sir Christopher Wren.

which he had little real sympathy; he drew out designs, which still exist, for converting Westminster Abbey into an Italian church, just as Inigo Jones had done with the exterior of the nave of old St. Paul's, but we cannot be too thankful that this suggestion was never carried out.

With King George III on the throne our ancestors contented themselves with dull, but substantial buildings of which some hard things have been written, but they were at least respectable and free from sham, while the churches, although not elegant, were well-built and occasionally picturesque, as we see by the perfect little building of this date at Billesley, near Stratford-on-Avon (91).

Later there came upon the scene two men who, by their combined influence, were destined to bring some kind of order out of chaos. Charles Barry and Welby Pugin were at once scholars and architects. Though the former **Barry and** rather favoured the classical style **Pugin.** he thoroughly understood the Gothic, while Pugin was a thorough mediaevalist, a true artist, and a bold exponent in his *Contrasts* of a complete return to mediaeval architecture as the only possible cure for the evils which had crept into the art of building.

Barry's idea, which was perhaps the more practical, was to correct by careful study the errors into which the later exponents of both Classic and Gothic architecture had fallen, and he endeavoured by well-thought-out modifications to evolve a style more suitable to modern requirements. Pugin, however, would have none of it, and although he supplied his friend with designs for the details and woodwork of the Houses of Parliament which Barry was building, they did not collaborate in any further way, and both died before the Houses of Parliament were completed, in which, as a matter of fact, Barry's complete and original scheme was but partly followed.

Pugin's earlier works were mostly Roman Catholic churches. In the Roman Catholic Cathedral of St. Chad, at Birmingham, there is a dignity, loftiness and simplicity surpassed by few Gothic buildings when that style was at its zenith.

Our best architects acknowledge that except by the adoption of new methods of building, originality in architecture is an impossibility, mainly because all the styles of the past have been worked out to their legitimate conclusion, and have been perfected under circumstances and conditions with which we have entirely broken ; the originality in detail which pervades and permeates our Gothic buildings and gives them the greater part of their charm, must, of necessity, be out of our reach unless we blend what we are pleased to call the practicality of our age, with a certain amount of that air of poetry and romance, religious fervour and devoutness, which animated the builders and craftsmen of the past.

Chapter IX.

Church Furniture and Accessories.

THE most important feature of the interior of a church is the altar. Altars of gold and brass formed a very important part of the furniture of both the Tabernacle of Moses and the Temple of Solomon; and almost every form of religion used a raised structure for sacrificial worship that corresponds more or less to the Christian altar. There is little doubt that in the early days of Christianity altars were made of wood, but the Council of Epone directed in A.D. 509, that " no altars should be consecrated with the chrism of holy oil, but such as were made of stone only." St. Augustine states (*Epist.* 185, *c.* 27) that they beat the Bishop Maximinianus

The Altar. with the wood of the altar under which he had taken refuge; and William of Malmesbury in his *Vita St. Wulstan*, says that St. Wulstan, when Bishop of Worcester, 1062-95, demolished throughout his diocese the wooden altars which were still in exis-tence in England.

One church, one altar, was the rule in early days, and Cardinal Bona states that he could find no evidences of a contrary practice " till the time of Gregory the Great, and then only in the Latin Church."

The custom of having subordinate altars arose in the days when the tomb of a saint or martyr was regarded as a fitting place for the celebration of the Eucharist. When stone altars were introduced, the relics of saints were enclosed within them, and bishops were threatened with deprivation of office should they consecrate churches without relics, a decree that holds good in the Roman Catholic Church to-day.

When the stone altar was displaced by the communion table, the latter generally occupied the position at the eastern end of the chancel vacated by the former, and this was the direction of the *Injunctions* (see Lansdowne MSS. 8, F. 16, British Museum), but there was no uniformity. This position gave umbrage to the Puritan mind, and resulted, during the Cromwellian period, in the communion table being placed in the centre of the chancel, with seats all round for the communicants ; an arrangement that survives in a few English churches and in Jersey ; but, generally speaking, the holy table was placed against the eastern wall of the chancel, where it remains to the present day, and this is still the usual position. At Winchcombe, Gloucester, in the eighteenth century, the altar stood centrally, with seats for the communicants on the south, east, and

Photograph

Sedilia and Chantry Chapel, St. Mary, Luton.

Fredk. Thurston, F.R.P.S.

(left) A rare instance of four-seated sedilia; (right) the beautiful little chapel of Barnard's chantry.

Photograph   *[by the Author*

Billesley, Warwickshire.
A church built entirely in the Georgian era.

north sides respectively. A similar arrangement existed at Deerhurst, near Tewkesbury, and does so still at Lyddington, in Rutland, while the central position has been reverted to in one modern London church, Professor Beresford Pite's building, Christ Church, Brixton Road.

In England altars were taken down about 1550, replaced in the reign of Mary, to be again removed in that of Elizabeth. So complete was their destruction on the last occasion, and in the devastations of the Puritans, that very few remain *in situ*. Pre-Reformation altar-slabs, however, are preserved among other places at Arundel Church and Westham, Sussex ; and in the ruined Church of St. Mary, at Ripon. The little chapels attached to hospitals or almshouses at Stamford, Glastonbury, Salisbury, and several other places have also retained their old altar-slabs. In the little church at Corton, near Upwey, Dorset, the old stone altar is intact, marked with the five crosses, and here as in other cases it is still *in situ*, although the top is covered by a board.

Portable or super-altars appear in certain circumstances to have been used for the celebration of mass. One of these made of jasper and of circular shape is in St. Albans Abbey, and another of silver was found in the coffin with the body of St. Cuthbert, when his grave was opened in 1827. Simon of Durham relates that when the remains of St. Acca were translated, a wooden table in the form of an altar was found upon the saint's breast, and Leland records that down to his day a portable altar, said to have been used by Bede, was kept at Jarrow.

Behind the altar it was usual to have a background—the reredos. In small churches the reredos is frequently little more than a panelled or decorated section of the east wall **The Reredos.** of the chancel against which the altar is placed. The decoration may be elaborate or otherwise, in stone or wood, and may contain niches or corbel brackets for images, or framework in which pictures are or have been placed. But in other examples the reredos may be a screen, the altar screen, in the true sense. The great stone screens at Winchester, St. Albans, Durham, Southwark and Christchurch are perhaps the finest expressions of this particular church detail. They have doorways on either side of the altar by which the priest could pass entirely round it when censing.

Wherever there was an altar there was close by a piscina in the form of a shallow stone basin or sink, with a drain to carry off **The** whatever was poured into it, so **Piscina.** that where all other trace of an altar has disappeared, its position is often proved by the presence of the piscina. It was used to receive the water in which the priest ceremonially washed his hands in mass at the " lavabo," as well as that used for the ablutions. It is usually found within a niche, although the basin frequently projects from the face of the wall, and is sometimes supported on a shaft rising from the floor. In the Early English and Decorated piscinas there are sometimes two basins and two drains, while a beautiful example of a double piscina is that in Lady St. Mary Church, Wareham. Within the niche a shelf is often found, on which the cruets for wine and water were placed before they were required at the altar. Piscinas are unknown in England before the middle of the twelfth century, and those of that date are rare, Of the thirteenth and succeeding centuries we have many good examples, in spite of the bad treatment they have received. Their forms and architectural settings vary greatly from a simple trefoil-headed niche to an elaborate composition, but the character of their details will always decide their approximate date.

An aumbry, recess, or small cupboard, used for the storing of the church plate, may still be seen in many churches. It is sometimes **The Aumbry.** found near the piscina, but more often on the opposite side of the chancel. A somewhat rare form of the aumbry is to be seen at St. Mary's Church, Sandwich, and at certain churches in Norfolk and Suffolk. These are often nearly twelve feet high, are very narrow in proportion to their height

and are usually supposed to have been for processional crosses. Dr. J. Charles Cox, however,
says they would be more rightly named banner-
stave lockers.

The sedilia, from the Latin *sedile*, a seat, is the
name given to the seats once used by the celebrant
Sedilia. and ministers during the pauses
in the mass. They were sometimes
moveable, but were, in this country, more usually
formed of masonry and recessed into the wall.
The seats are generally three in number, which,
in parish churches were for the priest, deacon, and
sub-deacon. We have a few examples of four-seated
sedilia, as at Luton Church (90) and Turvey,
Beds. ; Rothwell Church, Northants ; and elsewhere ; and a five-seated example at Southwell
Minster.

Occasionally we find the sedilia on both sides
of the chancel, as at the charming although re-
·stored Norman church of Hurstbourne Priors,
Hants ; a rarity which has been described not very
convincingly as nothing more than " an architectural conceit." Sometimes a long seat under
one arch is found, and when three seats are used
the two western ones are usually a little lower than
the eastern one. Numerous examples remain in
our churches, some being as early as the latter part
of the twelfth century, but the majority are later
and extend to the end of the Perpendicular period.
The seats are often separated by shafts, and or-

namented with panelling, niches, pinnacles, tabernacle work ; and crowned with canopies loaded with a wealth of beautiful detail.

Stalls are fixed seats in the choir, either wholly or partially enclosed, and appropriated for the use of those officiating in the services. Previous to the Reformation all large and many small churches had a range of wooden stalls on either side, and at **Stalls.** the west end of, the choir. In cathedrals they were usually enclosed at the back with panelling, and surmounted by overhanging canopies of tabernacle work, of which those in Henry VII's Chapel at Westminster, and in Winchester, Exeter and Manchester cathedrals are among our finest examples.

The misericord is a projecting block of wood, usually carved, found on the underside of the seat of a stall, and the seat being hinged it can be raised and the misericord used as a support, but at a higher level than the seat itself. The carvings (127) on them are very curious and interesting, and among our best examples are those at Christchurch Priory, Exeter Cathedral, St. Botolph's, Boston, and Henry VII's Chapel, Westminster.

In former times pulpits were placed in the nave, attached to a wall, pillar, or screen, and frequently against the second pier from the chancel arch. Some are of wood, others of stone ; the former being sometimes of polygonal shape, with foliage or tracery in the panels. Few exist of earlier date than the Perpendicular period, but stone pulpits of Decorated date are sometimes found, as in the refectory of the Abbey at Beaulieu, Hants, now used as the parish church, a very early specimen. The majority of wooden pulpits are hexagonal or octagonal ; some stand on slender shafts, others on stone bases (103). A few Post-Reformation ones have canopies or sounding boards, and their dates can be fixed by the style and character of their ornament. At

Pulpits. Kenton, Devon, as in a score of other examples, the pulpit has retained its original paintings. Jacobean pulpits are very numerous, and are sometimes gilded or painted. Croscombe Church, Somerset, is full of Jacobean work including a very beautiful pulpit.

Apart from their architectural qualities many old pulpits have great historical interest. For instance, in the little church at Broadwindsor, Dorset, the fine Jacobean pulpit from which that quaint old divine, Thomas Fuller, preached many an eloquent sermon, may still be seen. Besides being placed in churches, pulpits were erected in the refectories of monastic houses, as the one just mentioned, at Beaulieu, while the old pulpit of Shrewsbury Abbey now stands in the station yard of that interesting town. Again pulpits were occasionally erected for open-air preaching. The best remembered open-air pulpit was that at Paul's Cross in St. Paul's churchyard, London, which has long disappeared, but that at Magdalen College, Oxford, is well known. In mediæval days open-air pulpits were also erected near the roads, on bridges and on the steps of market and other crosses, some of the latter being still known as preaching crosses of which good examples remain at Hereford and at Iron Acton, Gloucester. The fashion has been revived in recent years and good modern open-air pulpits may be seen at St. Martin's, the old parish church of Birmingham ; at St. James', Piccadilly ; St. Mary's, Whitechapel ; Holy Trinity, Marylebone ; the parish church of Spitalfields ; St. Bartholomew's, Bethnal Green, and in other places.

Open-air Pulpits.

In many churches there will be found a screen (102) dividing the chancel—that portion of the church reserved for those who officiate—from the nave—the portion of the church open to the public. Often above this screen there was a small gallery — known as the rood-loft. Access to the rood-loft was obtained by a narrow staircase inside the church. In the vast majority of cases the entrance and exit to such openings were within the church itself, though there are also occasional instances where there was an opening in the outside wall.

Screens and Rood-lofts.

G

The object of the screen does not lend itself to discussion—its purpose was to screen off the chancel. The rood-loft has been the subject of many different explanations, but it is now generally admitted that it was used for musical purposes. Mr. A. Hamilton Thompson, F.S.A., says for instance : " the habitual use of the loft was as an organ gallery." and Dr. J. Charles Cox, says : " Broadly speaking, the common use of a rood-loft . . . . . was that of a music gallery." It is, however, certain that in some rood-lofts there was an altar, and piscinas remain in some few churches in such positions as to prove this.

In the great monastic churches the custom was to have two screens. The first from the west was the rood-screen, and possessed two doorways. The second, farther eastward, was the choir-screen. This possessed only a central doorway which gave access to the choir. The term *pulpitum* was apparently used for any loft whether above the rood-screen or choir-screen. In parish churches, however, the chancel-screen did duty for both rood-screen and choir-screen. Modern usage applies the term pulpitum to the choir-screen still existing in our greater churches. The pulpitum is often called a *Jubé*, because in singing the gospel the deacon first sang the request *Jube, domine, benedicere.* The benediction of the Sacrament was often given from the pulpitum. A good example of the pulpitum may be seen at Christchurch.

Screens are of stone or wood. In construction the wooden screen generally consists of a series of vertical members, framed into a sill piece, and connected at the head with a beam or platform upon which is planted the elaborately wrought cornice. About four feet six inches from the floor level a horizontal member or transom is usually framed and the whole of these members are moulded more or less elaborately. The portion from the floor to the transom, on each side of the central door, is filled with panels, upon which tracery heads, and figures of saints were occasionally fixed or painted. Mr. Francis Bond (*Screens and Galleries in English Churches*) defines two types— the Norfolk type, common in East Anglia, and the Devon type, characteristic of the West Country. In later centuries when chancel arches were omitted —the building forming one great hall—the aisles were often continuous, and the screen continued across both aisles .

Screens are frequently found constructed of stone, though they are comparatively rare in parish churches. Beautiful examples of the fourteenth century exist at Great Bardfield and Stebbing, Essex, though these are exceptional in form, consisting of triple arches carried from the floor to the head of the chancel arch. At Totnes, Devon, there is one built by the Corporation in 1459. In cathedral and large conventual churches stone screen work is very general.

In parish churches the chancel screen also served, in the majority of instances, to support the rood, and the top of the screen would generally consist of a substantial platform or loft carried on a double bracketted cornice. Sometimes, however, there would be no loft and if the screen were insufficiently strong a special rood beam would bear the image of the crucified Christ.

The parish churches of England retain a greater proportionate number of these screens than the churches on the continent. They are to be found in every county, though the counties of Devonshire and Cornwall, and Norfolk and Suffolk are pre-eminently the counties for screens (102). Of rood-lofts examples remain at (*inter alia*), Long Sutton, Banwell, Dunster, Norton-Fitzwarren and Mine-head, Somerset ; Newark, Notts ; Uffculme, Cullompton, Kenton (102), Plymtree, Staverton and Hartland, Devon ; Mere, Wilts ; and Hubberholme, Yorks. Rood-beams are rarely to be found, though the corbels which supported them may often be seen and occasionally projecting portions of the beams from which the middle has been sawn away are also to be found. There is one example of a rood-beam *in situ* at Tunstead, Norfolk (this is painted). There are others in Norfolk and there is one at Cullompton in Devon, while at Old Shoreham, Sussex, there is a massive beam carved with Norman moulding, facing the nave, and above the Norman archway into the central tower, which

Dr. Cox suggests may have supported a rood. No single example of the rood itself remains. They were all destroyed at the Reformation, but at Cullompton, Devon, the base of the cross—a carved Calvary—is preserved. In some cases the rood was painted on a board or tympanum, which fitted the upper part of the chancel arch, and some of these paintings have been discovered and preserved by restoration. A notable instance is that of Wenhaston, Suffolk. The screen tympanum here is now fixed above a west gallery. In a very few other cases the tympanum has been preserved.

Much screenwork will be found, especially in large churches and cathedrals, though also often in parish churches, separating the choirs from the choir aisles, enclosing chantry chapels and dividing subordinate portions of the church from the main body. These are termed parclose screens and used as such we frequently find portions of a displaced chancel screen. In Paignton Church, Devon, is a very fine example of a stone parclose screen.

In many of the old churches the font is the sole remaining piece of ancient furniture and in some instances it is the only link with an **The Font.** earlier church that once stood upon the same site. For example, it is not an uncommon thing to find a font of Norman date in a church every portion of which belongs to a

later period of architecture. The earliest font, as
we now understand the term, was a low tub-like
vessel (31) standing on the floor, soon to be raised on
a low base, then on several shafts and finally on a
pedestal (106) (see *Fonts and Font Covers*, by
Francis Bond).

In the same book, Mr. Francis Bond traces the
conversion of pagan altars, Roman columns, and
the shafts of Christian crosses into fonts, of which
last there are examples at Dolton Church, Devon ;
and Melbury Bubb, Dorset ; both of which are
made up of fragments of early churchyard crosses.
The curious projecting basin near the rim of the
font, as found at Youlgreave, Derbyshire, was once
thought to have been provided for holding the
cruet of holy oil ; but was probably intended to
carry off the water which dripped from the child's
head, as this water was not allowed to fall into
the font again. Where no provision was made
on the font for this purpose a portable basin
would be used, and in the wills of the fourteenth
and fifteenth centuries " silver font-bowls " are
often bequeathed to churches.

Good examples of pre-Conquest fonts bearing inscriptions are those at Potterne, Wilts ; Bridekirk,
Cumberland ; and Little Billing, Northants ; while
probably of this period also are those of Deerhurst,
Gloucester (106) ; and Bucknell, Salop ; but with a
large number of rude and early examples it is not
possible to say definitely whether they belong to

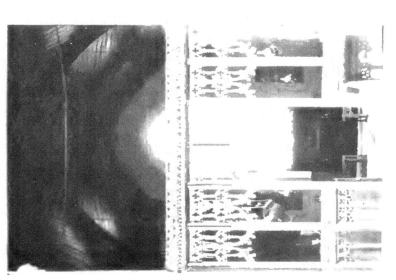

Two Typical Screens.

(a) The East Anglian type: Barningham, Norfolk. (b) The Devon type: Kenton, Devon.

Photograph H. Montague Cooper

Trull Church, Somerset.

Famed for its wood carving illustrated in the screens, the pulpit, and
the bench ends.

the pre- or post-Conquest periods. For many years the bowl of the Deerhurst font was in use at a farmhouse, whence it was rescued in 1845 and placed in Longdon Church, Worcestershire, where it remained until 1870, when the discovery of the stem resulted in the complete font being restored to Deerhurst. The leaden font at Barnetby-le-Wold, Lincolnshire, was found some years ago in the church coal-house, and large numbers of fonts have known long periods of disuse since the Reformation. It may be taken as a general rule that if a font is found eastward of the centre of the nave it has been removed from its original position.

Of Norman fonts we have a large number. Some of these are plain hollow cylinders ; others are massive squares borne on a large central stem and on small shafts at the corners. Of this type the Winchester font is a good example. It is made of Tournai marble and is one of several in the kingdom, the others being at St. Peter, Ipswich ; Lincoln Minster and Thornton Curtis. Lincs. ; St. Michael, Southampton, East Meon, and St. Mary Bourne, Hants.* Norman fonts show more than those of any other period the favourite legends of the age. One would think that the symbols of baptism would have been the fitting form of decoration for fonts ; but the Norman sculptor had no thoughts in this direction, such carvings being the exception.

* See *Black Tournai Fonts in England*, by Cecil H. Eden

Although the canon required the font to be of stone we have some twenty-nine leaden fonts in our churches, among them those at Barnetby-le-Wold, Lincolnshire ; Wareham, Dorset ; Walton-on-the-Hill, Surrey ; Edburton, Parham, and Pyecombe, Sussex ; and a very fine one at Brookland, in Romney Marsh, Kent. Siston Church in Gloucestershire, has a leaden font of late Norman design. Other examples are at Slimbridge (dated 1664), Sandhurst, Frampton-on-Severn, Tidenham, Down Hatherley, and Oxenhall, all in Gloucestershire.

The later Norman and Early English fonts are mostly octagonal, a form that was generally retained through the Decorated and Perpendicular periods, although there are Decorated fonts of hexagonal form at Rolvenden, Kent and Heckington, Lincolnshire. It is rather singular that although the Decorated era produced so many beautiful churches, the fonts lack the vitality of those of the Norman and the grace of those of the Early English periods. It is quite certain that the various shapes given to fonts had originally no symbolical meaning whatever. The symbolists gave mystical meanings of the shapes *after* and not before these had been determined by more urgent conditions.

Good examples of seventeenth century fonts and their covers are those of St. Stephen, Walbrook ; St. Katherine Cree, Leadenhall Street, St. Andrew Undershaft, St. Mary Axe ; and All

Hallows Barking, Great Tower Street, all four in London ; the last two fonts are the work of Nicholas Stone, whose finest example is thought to be that of Great Stanmore, Middlesex, dated 1634.

As fonts were kept filled with water a covering became essential for keeping it fresh and clean. **Font Covers.** Edmund, Archbishop of Canterbury (1236), directed that fonts should be covered and locked, and the reason assigned by Lyndwode is *propter sortilegia*—to avoid magic influences. The font cover from being a plain lid, developed into a highly ornamental feature enriched with pinnacles, crockets, and all the other architectural conceits of the day. The elaborate and well known examples at Ufford, Suffolk, and North Walsham, Norfolk, may be instanced. Of the former the notorious William Dowsing reported : " There is a glorious cover over the font like a Pope's triple crown, with a Pelican pecking its breast, all gilt over with gold." Representations of the " Pelican in her Piety," or, heraldically expressed, the Pelican vulning herself, in order to feed her young with the blood of her breast, were frequently used as an emblem of Christ.

Devonshire has a few good font covers, as at Pilton and Cockington,though as compared with the amount of beautiful screen-work in the county, the font covers are meagre both in design and numbers. A good inscribed example is that at Tuxford, Notts, dated 1673. Taken as a whole our parish churches have retained a large number of these interesting specimens of woodwork.

Two curious examples, which embrace the font itself, are those at Littlebury and Thaxted, Essex, and two of the most beautiful are at Heston and Littleton, in Middlesex. All Hallows Barking, has a very elaborate font cover, hung in 1685, which has been attributed to Grinling Gibbons. It is of wood with fruit and flowers supported by cupids over whom is perched the holy dove.

In exceedingly rare instances, as at Luton, Beds; and Trunch, Norfolk (107), we find the font placed within an elaborate canopy; while at Canterbury it is placed in a small circular building called the Bell Jesus. The Luton example in St. Mary's Church, is described fully in the Homeland Handbook, No. 47. It is of stone, in the Decorated style, dates from the time of Edward III, and is said to have been designed by William of Wykeham for Queen Philippa. That of St. Botolph, Trunch, Norfolk, consists of an elaborate wooden canopy supported on six slender pillars. The lower surface of the upper works, forming a roof to the font enclosure is a fine specimen of fan-tracery. This is surmounted by an open crocketed canopy formerly terminated by a finial of which only the base remains.

Squints or hagioscopes are oblique openings driven through walls or piers so that a view of the

FONTS

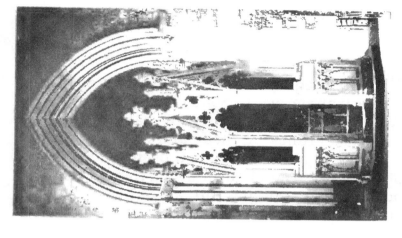

Font Covers.

(a) St. Peter, Sudbury, Suffolk; (b) Trunch, Norfolk; (c) Luton, Beds.

altar may be obtained from places where it would
Squints. otherwise be obscured. They are of
frequent occurrence in our churches
and are very numerous in South Wales, Devon, and
the West generally. They rarely have ornament,
but are sometimes arched and enriched with
tracery, and in addition to their occurrence on one
or both sides of the chancel arch, they are found
in rooms above porches, in aisles, side-chapels,
and the like.

Holy water stoups are generally small niches
with stone basins formed in the wall either within
Stoups. or just outside the porch. They also
occur inside the buildings, but are
rarely found unmutilated. An unusual form occurs
at Wootton Courtney, Somerset (148).

Bench ends carved with a variety of symbolical
or secular devices are very common in Somerset,
Devon and Cornwall, so common that it is rare
to enter a church in either of these counties
without finding one or more. The bench ends of
Norfolk and Suffolk are also very
Bench ends. numerous. Among the best sets are
those at Barwick, Spaxton, and Trull
(103), Somerset ; Ottery St. Mary, East Budleigh
and Sutcombe, Devon ; while for workmanship
those of Mullion, Cornwall, take high rank. At Kilk-
hampton and at Morwenstow in this county are to
be seen also some notable examples. The church
of East Budleigh alone has over sixty of these

carved bench ends, one of which bears the arms of Raleigh (who was born at Hayes Barton, near by) impaling those of Grenville.

The right of a fugitive to claim protection from the vengeance of his enemies dates back to long before the Christian era. The right of sanctuary originally inhered in every church and churchyard but in later days it became in practice more commonly claimed at the sanc- tuaries such as Durham, Beverley, Westminster, etc., which were speci- ally chartered. The common law protection afforded by a sanctuary was briefly that " a person accused of felony might save his life by entering a sanctuary, and there before a coroner, within forty days, confess the felony and take an oath of abjuration entailing banishment, except always those guilty of sacrilege or high treason." The banished refugee, cross in hand and clothed in sackcloth was sent along the highways to a specified port to take the first ship to the continent. The right of claiming the privilege of sanctuary extended to all classes, from the lowest criminal to the highest noble, and on more than one occasion members of the reigning house have repaired to such a place in times of trouble. The right continued unimpaired down to the Reformation, by which time these shelters had become so numerous and were so much re- sorted to by criminals, that after various Acts of

The right of Sanctuary.

Parliament had curtailed their privileges, they were nearly all abolished during the reign of James I, although the right continued to hold good in a few isolated cases as protection from civil process. Various churches in England claim to possess sanctuary rings, in respect of which there is a general belief

Sanctuary Rings that the criminal reaching sanctuary had only to clasp the ring to secure immunity. There is a certain amount of evidence that the knocker

Durham Sanctuary Knocker

at Durham Cathedral was used at night to awaken two custodians, who slept in the church that entrance might be accorded to fugitives arriving by night. There is a good deal yet to be learned concerning this subject and it is perhaps safer at present to question the authenticity of other cases in which a like claim is made. The Durham ring consists of a dragon's head, quite hollow inside, the rims of the eyes showing traces of the enamel with which they were once filled. The head measures $10\frac{1}{2}$ inches across and two feet over the radiating mane, the material being bronze.

Chapter X.

Bells and Belfries.

WITH the pre-Christian history and uses of bells we are not here concerned. We do know, however, that they were used in the early days of Christianity to summon the people to worship, and they will show you at the reputed Saxon church of St. Martin, at Wareham, a small door in the wall of the chancel which was always opened when the bells began to ring, so that the devil could escape from the building. We need not argue as to whether the bells worn by the High Priest (*Exodus* xxviii, 33, 35) were bells at all ; nor is it essential for our purpose to know whether bells were invented in China and imported into India, or *vice versa*. As the late Rev. H. R. Haweis says :" It is enough to note that small bells preceded large ones, although large bells are generally held to have been used in India and China long before they reached Europe, but if, as Cardinal Manning has recently reminded us, the history of European civilization is the history of the church, it is equally true that the history of the church—I might add the state—is inseparably bound up with the history of bells."

Monastic Bells.

That bells were early used for ecclesiastical purposes in England has been recorded by Bede, who, speaking of the death of St. Hilda, A.D. 680, says that " one of the sisters in the distant monastery of Hackness, thought she heard as she slept, the sound of the bell which called them to prayers," and Abbot Turketyl gave to Crowland Abbey a great bell called Guthlac, and afterwards six others which he called Bartholomew and Butelin, Turketyl and Tatwin, and Pega and Bega. St. Dunstan gave bells to many of the churches in Somerset, and he also seems to have introduced bell ringing into the monasteries.

A few words may be of interest concerning the number and purposes of these monastic bells, with which the life of the monks must have been completely bound up. The *Signum* woke up the whole community at daybreak. The *Squilla* announced the frugal meal in the refectory ; but for those working in the gardens, the cloister-bell, or *Campanella*, was rung. The abbot's *Cordon*, or handbell, summoned the brothers and novices to their Superior ; whilst the *Petasius* was used to call in those working at a distance from the main building. At bed-time the *Tiniolum* was sounded, and the *Noctula* was rung at intervals throughout the night to call the monks to watch and pray. The *Corrigiumcula* was the scourging bell, while the sweet-toned *Nota*, a choir bell, was rung at the consecration of the elements.

The use of the bell-tower was recognised in the ancient Saxon law, which gave the title of thane to anyone who had a church with a bell-tower on his estate.

The campanile of old St. Paul's was a detached one, the bell of which, Sir Laurence Gomme tells us, summoned the citizens to the folk-moot. Markland tells us that "the great bell-tower which once formed part of the abbey church of St. Edmundsbury was commenced about 1436. From the year 1441 to 1500 legacies were still being given towards the building. In 1461 an individual, probably a benefactor, desired to be buried *in magno ostio novi campanilis.*" Salisbury Cathedral once possessed a fine detached campanile that stood until 1789. Judged from old prints, it appears to have been of the same period as the chapter-house and cloisters. The stone tower was in two storeys with lancet windows in the lower, and traceried ones above, with a wooden spire capping the whole. In 1553 the Commissioners reported that a peal of ten bells remained. Two of these, the seventh and eighth, were recast in 1680, and the sixth is the present clock bell of the cathedral. What became of the others is unknown.

One of the most beautiful campaniles or bell-towers still standing is that at Evesham, in Worcestershire, which is a good specimen of Perpendicular architecture. It was built by Abbot Lichfield, the last abbot but one of the abbey, and took six years in building, and was not quite completed when the famous abbey, of which it was a final ornament, was pulled down.

In addition to this Evesham example we have many detached bell-towers, as at Garway, Herefordshire, which is joined to the nave only by a narrow passage. Beccles, in Suffolk, has a very fine example, Perpendicular in style, and with a series of buttresses, rising in diminishing stages almost up to the coping-stone. At the fine church of St. Mary, East Bergholt, Suffolk, the bell-tower was never finished, and the bells still hang in a wooden belfry cage in the churchyard, which was no doubt intended originally as a temporary shelter.

Detached bell-towers.

One of the most curious instances of an isolated belfry is that at Warmsworth, near Doncaster, which stands in the village, more than half-a-mile away from the church. The result is that the bell ceases to ring a quarter of an hour before the services begin to enable the ringer to get to the church in time.

There are many other examples of detached bell-towers remaining, as at Chichester, Sussex; West Walton, East Dereham, and Little Snoring, Norfolk; Berkeley, Gloucester; Elstow, Bedfordshire; Ledbury, Herefordshire; and two very curious ones at Pembridge and Yarpole, in the same county. In the Fenland district alone we

H

find examples at Wisbech, Fleet, Whaplode, Sutton St. Mary, Terrington St. Clement, and Terrington St. John, either now or originally detached. Sussex has three examples, and Herefordshire seven, but wherever placed, the tower in Herefordshire is generally remarkable for its position. In all there are between thirty and forty English churches where the bell-tower stands isolated from the rest of the fabric.

Although those at Beccles and Evesham are very good, they are probably not equal to those of West Walton, Norfolk, and Berkeley, Gloucester ; and of these two West Walton takes first place. This tower stands on four great arches, which serve as a kind of lych-gate and entrance to the church-yard. It is lavishly arcaded and has large belfry windows with pierced circular openings above the heads of the two pointed lights enclosed under a single arch. It is a fine example of ripe Early English work.

Closely connected with bells and belfries are the bell-gables or bell-turrets, so frequently found at the west ends of our smaller churches which have no towers. They are for instance very common in

Bell-turrets. the case of the West Surrey churches. The whole of this district forming part of the forest of Windsor and consist-ting largely of heathland, was poor and sparsely inhabited. As a rule, therefore, the churches are small and they carry these bell-cots instead of being provided with external towers. Bell-cots usually contain but one bell, but are sometimes found with two, and at Radipole Church, near Weymouth, the bell-turret was originally designed to carry three bells. They are generally most picturesque little features of which a few may be of Norman date, but by far the greater number of them are Early English, a style in which they are frequently found. One sometimes finds a similar, but smaller, erection at the eastern end of the roof of the nave, but this was used for a very different purpose, for while the bell at the western end was rung to summon the parishioners to service, that at the eastern end, known as the sanctus or mass-bell, was rung at the elevation of the host during the celebration of mass. The sanctus bell was not however always placed on the apex of the roof; it sometimes occupied a position in the lantern or tower, or in a turret of larger dimensions. At Barnstaple and in other places the sanctus bell is hung under a tiny cot projecting from the spire. The portable sanctus bell was always rung by the server at the altar at various parts of the mass, but where there was also an exterior sanctus bell, that also was rung at the elevation in answer to the handbell at the altar, in order that invalids and others unable to attend mass might join in the act of adoration.

It was long a reproach to our country churches that they possessed no perfect chime of bells, such for example, as those to be heard in so many parts

of Belgium.   In 1889, however, a fine carillon of
bells was placed in the tower of Cattistock Church,
Dorset, a stately modern building designed by
Scott.   The bells hang on a wooden frame independent of the tower walls, so that the vibration
shall not injure the fabric.   The chime is probably the only perfect one to be found in England,
and it was inaugurated by the famous carilloneur
of Malines, M. Joseph Denyn, who comes periodi-
cally to this Dorset village, the church of which
can be seen from the railway line at Maiden
Newton, to give recitals and change or modify the
tunes.   Since their original hanging nine of the
bells (the whole carillon consists of thirty-five) have
been recast at the celebrated foundry of M. Felix
van Aerschodt, at Louvain.   This carillon owes
its being to a former rector, the Rev. Keith H.
Barnes, who, together with the members of
his family, bore the heavy cost of the under-
taking.

Bell inscriptions are very interesting, and although an immense number have been printed at
various times, much remains to be done if a complete record is to be made.   There is scarcely a
brass in the country that has not been rubbed,
some of them dozens of times, but the bell-hunter
is not much in evidence, which is not a matter for
surprise to those who have made a perilous ascent
into an old bell chamber, and seen the accumulated
dust of centuries.   Bell inscriptions bear a great

family likeness, and in this matter at any rate the ancient bell-founders were great plagiarists.

The following specimens of inscriptions are from the bells at Clifford Chambers, an interesting little village near Stratford-on-Avon.   The bells number five, and were recast in 1771-3 by the Bagleys, the famous bell-founders of Chalcombe, Gloucestershire.

1.   I.M.B MADE : ME : THE : LEADER · OF : THIS : PEAL : TO : BE.   1771.

2.   M. BAGLEY : MADE : ME : 1771 : JOHN : SMITH : WILLIAM . COOKS : CHURCH : WARDENS.

3.   M.B MADE : MEE : 1771 : JOHN : SMITH : WILLIAM : COOKS : C.W.

4.   JOHN : SMITH : WILLIAM : COOKS : CHURCH : WARDENS : WILLIAM : BAGLEY : MADE : MEE : 1771.

5.   AND : NOW : I : HOP : TO : PLEASE : YOU : ALL : AND . SING : TO : THE : GREAT : CREATERS : PRAYS : MY : FATE : HATH : BEEN : UNFORTUNATE : BEE : FOAR : MY : SELF : COULD : RAIS : MATTHEW : BAGLEY : MADE : MEE : 1773.

Chapter XI.

The Spire: Its Origin and Development.

PROBABLY the most beautiful feature of a Gothic church is the spire, which soaring above the town or village forms a prominent landmark, denoting the location of the House of God. Although found occasionally in other styles, the spire is essentially Gothic, and one of the most marked characteristics of this period. Most spires fall into two classes, those constructed of timber and covered with slates, lead, tiles or shingles, and those built of stone or brick. Examples of both kinds are very numerous on the continent and in England, while shingle spires are especially common in Sussex.

The spire is generally acknowledged to have originated from the small pyramidal roof so frequently found on Saxon and Norman towers. This gradually became elongated, and the towers were sometimes gabled on each side, although the only instance of this in England is the remarkable Saxon tower at Sompting, Sussex. This shows us very clearly the angles of the spire resting upon the apex of each

Saxon and Norman.

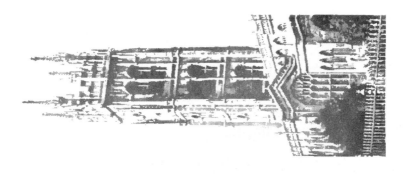

(a) Boston, Lincs.

Notable Towers.

(b) St. Clement, Sandwich

(c) St. Mary Magdalene, Taunton

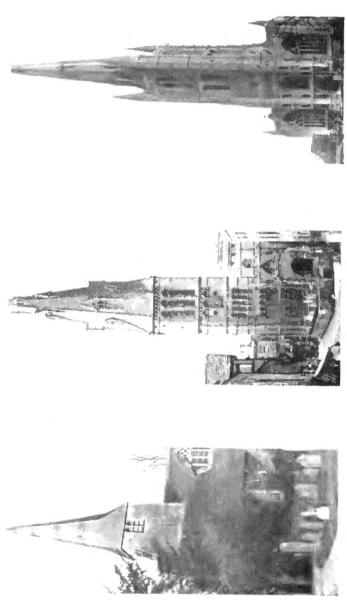

Examples of Spires.

a) A shingled broach spire (Early English), Tandridge, Surrey.   (*b*) A broach spire of the Decorated period, St. Mary, Stamford.   (*c*) A magnificent parapetted and crocketted spire, St. Wulfram, Grantham.

Photographs: Homeland Copyright, H. Walker, and A. M. Emary.

gable, so that the spire itself is set obliquely to the square of the tower.

Saxon and Norman spires are very rare in England, Sompting being our best example of the former and those on the eastern transepts of Canterbury Cathedral of the latter. Barnack Church, in Northamptonshire, has a curious spire showing the transition from Norman to Early English.

Of Early English spires we have, fortunately, some good examples, among which are those at Oxford Cathedral, Wilford and Wansted, in the same county and a very graceful one at Leighton Buzzard. These thirteenth century spires are very common in France, as at Chartres and St. Pierre, Caen.

Of fourteenth century, or Decorated, spires, we have many examples, of which perhaps the best is the beautiful spire of Salisbury Cathedral, although the fine one at St. Mary's, Oxford, runs it close for premier position. Two of the triple group **Decorated.** at Lichfield Cathedral belong to this period, as do those at Ross, (Hereford), Heckington. Stamford (119) and Grantham (119) (Lincs.), Newark (Notts,), King's Sutton (Northants), Bloxham (Oxon), and Snettisham (Norfolk). A peculiarity of the Salisbury spire is that it formed no part of the original design of the cathedral, having been added seventy years later. It is the loftiest spire in England—404 feet—about forty feet higher than the cross of St. Paul's. It speaks well for the Gothic builders that such a vast superstructure as this tower and spire could be imposed upon walls and piers never intended to bear it.   At an early period it was found to have deflected twenty-three inches from the perpendicular, but there has been no sign of any further movement.

The spire, although less commonly used than formerly, was by no means abandoned by the builders of the Perpendicular period, **Perpendicular** and beautiful examples are those **spires.** at St. Michael's, Coventry, Kettering church, Northants ; and Rotherham Church, Yorkshire.   Those at Rotherham and Kettering are crocketted up the angles.   Unlike numerous examples in the two previous styles, Perpendicular spires spring from within the parapet and do not project over the external wall of the tower.   In many instances they were erected a considerable time after the construction of the towers on which they are placed.

It will be noticed that the sides of a church spire are often slightly curved, so as to swell out a little in the middle.   This is called the entasis and is necessary to correct the appearance of concavity which absolutely straight lines produce, as is well known to students of optics.   Where the spire has no entasis this effect is counteracted by the introduction of small projecting gables, bands of carving, crockets, or a little coronal.

One of the most clearly marked differences between English and continental spires is that the latter are much shorter than the towers which support them, the towers as a rule, being twice as high as the spires. In England, on the contrary, the spire is generally very much loftier than the tower. At Shottesbrook, Berks, and Ledbury, Herefordshire, the spires occupy as much as three-fifths of the total elevation, and the usual rule in England is for the tower to be a little less in height than the spire.

The masons lavished an extraordinary amount of care and skill on their spires. So much is this the case that there is hardly a mediæval spire in the country which can be called ill-designed or displeasing.

Church spires are very common in some counties and very rare in others. There are, of course, exceptions, but it is in flat districts that spires are most frequent, the most beautiful ones being found in Northamptonshire, Leicestershire, Lincolnshire, Warwickshire, Staffordshire, Nottinghamshire and Oxfordshire.

The top of the spire is frequently capped with a weather vane terminating in a cock. The custom of using a cock as the flag of the vane is of very early date, for Wolfstan, in his life of St. Ethelwold, written towards the end of the tenth century, speaks of one which surmounted Winchester Cathedral. In the Bayeux Tapestry one is shown

on the gable of Westminster Abbey, and one of
the early popes ordained that every church under
the papal jurisdiction should be surmounted by
a cock as emblematical of the sovereignty of the
church over the whole world.

It may seem a pity to disturb popular traditions,
but the spire, although peculiar to Christian architecture, has no inherent symbolism. It has
a climatic rather than a symbolical origin. The
pitch of the tower roof was gradually steepened
so that it could better carry off the snow and rain
so prevalent in northern lands. The small and
steeply-pitched tower roof was a utilitarian feature
only until the devotional art of the fourteenth and
fifteenth centuries caught at the idea, and developed it magnificently into the beautiful and
elongated spire that has become so distinctive and
suggestive a feature of our Christian churches.

Chapter XII.

Crypts.

THE crypts found beneath the choirs of several of
our cathedrals and abbeys, and in rare instances
under our churches, rarely extend beyond the
choir or chancel and its aisles, and are sometimes
of very small dimensions. They are often coeval
with the upper parts of the building, and although
not so elaborate in ornamentation as the fabric
they support, they are almost without exception
well constructed and well finished pieces of building. In some cases the crypt is of much older date
than any portion of the superstructure, as is the
case at York, Worcester and Rochester Cathedrals.
During the twelfth and thirteenth centuries the
roofs were often richly vaulted, and upheld by
cylindrical columns or clustered piers, furnished
with handsome bases and decorated capitals.
There is abundant evidence that crypts were at
one time furnished with altars, piscinas, and the
various fittings requisite for the celebration of mass,
and were also used as sepulchres, wherein the
shrines of relics and martyrs were carefully preserved. Of Saxon origin are the crypts at Ripon

Cathedral, Hexham Abbey and Repton Church, Derbyshire. The Ripon example is a plain barrel-vaulted chamber, about 11 feet long and 8 feet wide, with no pillars or ornament of any kind. It is popularly known as St. Wilfred's Needle, but the origin of the name is lost in obscurity. The Hexham crypt is very similar in character, but is somewhat longer, being more than 13 feet long and 8 feet wide. As at Ripon, there are hollows or shallow niches in the walls. The third Saxon crypt is that at Repton, but it has little in common with the other two. Its superficial area is nearly twice as great and the roof is supported on four columns, with plain square capitals rudely carved, and bearing much similarity to early Norman work. Hornsea Church, Yorks, has a very similar crypt to those above mentioned.

The position of the crypt varies. At Hereford Cathedral it is under the Lady Chapel, while at Lastingham, in Yorkshire, the crypt extends under the whole of the church, including the apse. At Wells the crypt is beneath the chapter-house, and Durham Cathedral has three crypts, one under what was the dormitory, another beneath the refectory, and the third under the prior's chapel. Of crypts of Norman date we have several examples, of which, perhaps, our best are those at Gloucester, Worcester, Canterbury and Winchester Cathedrals, while Canterbury is probably the largest of them all. Good crypts are also found at Wim-

borne Minster, Christchurch Priory, Fountains
Abbey (126), and St. Peter's-in-the-East, Oxford.

The Wimborne crypt is lighted by four windows.
The vaulting is supported by two pairs of pillars
which form three aisles, each of three bays. Mr.
Perkins, in his book on Wimborne Minster, says,
" On each side of the place where the altar stood
there are openings into the choir aisles. The exteriors of these are of the same form and size as the
crypt windows, but they are deeply splayed inside,
and probably were used as hagioscopes or squints,
to allow those kneeling in the choir aisles to see
the priest celebrating mass at the crypt altar."
It should be mentioned that the choir of Wimborne Minster is placed at a considerably higher
level than the choir aisles, which explains the unusual construction. The crypt at Christchurch is
of Norman date, and now serves as a vault for the
Malmesbury family.

The crypt of Canterbury Cathedral is claimed
and justly claimed, perhaps, as the largest and most
beautiful in England. It is thought to contain
fragments of Roman and Saxon work, and much
of it dates from the days of St. Anselm (1096-1100).
That portion of the crypt beneath the choir was
built by Prior Ernwulf and remains unaltered from
before the time of Becket's primacy. It was here
that the remains of St. Thomas à Becket lay from
1170 to 1220, and " here that Henry II, fasting
and discrowned, with naked feet, bared back, and

streaming tears, performed on July 12th, 1174, the memorable penance for his share in the murder of the great archbishop." The site of the shrine is still indicated by two columns which were placed at its head and foot respectively to support the crypt-vaulting, when the choir was rebuilt after the fire of 1174. A contemporary picture of Becket's original shrine, showing the oval openings through which the pilgrims kissed the bones, is on a piece of painted glass in the Trinity Chapel.

The Crypt at Fountains Abbey, Yorkshire.

A fine example of ribbed vaulting (Early English period)

EXAMPLES OF GROTESQUES

(*a*) Misericord at Sherborne Abbey.
(*b*) Dripstone Terminal: St. Mary, Beverley.
Photographs by the Author and by E. C. Seare.

Chapter XIII.

Painted Glass.

WINDOWS of painted glass are of much later date
than those of coloured or stained glass, for the
last named were used certainly in Byzantine, and
possibly in Roman days. These windows of
stained glass consisted mainly of a mosaic of
colours, and in character they were probably
much like the stained glass windows used in Con-
stantinople at the present day, the pattern being
formed by the traceried framework in which the
pieces of glass are inserted. Windows of this
kind are mentioned as early as the fifth century,
but those of painted glass not until the eighth.
There is evidence of a painted window having
Early. been placed in the Abbey of Te-
Painted Glass. gernsee, in Bavaria, in 999, and of
one set up in the French abbey of
Loroux in 1121. To 1137-40 belong those in the
apse of St. Denis, of which portions inscribed with
the name of Abbot Suger, still remain. It is
reasonable therefore to suppose that painted, as
distinct from stained glass, was employed in this
country shortly after the last-named date, although
our oldest known examples, those in Canterbury

Cathedral, belong to the latter end of the twelfth century.

We may safely assume that at this period glass painting was widely known in cathedral and conventual churches, though it was not until the century following that the painted window came into general use. The primary use of a window, whether glazed or not, is to admit light to the building in which it is placed. At the same time the wind, dust, and rain have to be kept out. In early days, before the general use of glass, this was accomplished by filling the window with a material which would keep out the rain without excluding all the light. In Italy thin slices of talc, marble, or alabaster were so used, but in northern lands vellum, or linen, were more frequently employed. It is quite possible, and indeed highly probable, that the earliest painted windows were those of parchment or linen. The monks accustomed to painting and illuminating manuscripts, and engrossing documents, would be led, almost instinctively, to decorate in a bolder and broader manner, the surfaces of the pieces of linen they stretched over their windows, and the desire to decorate coloured glass, in a similar manner, when such came into general use, would be irresistible. However, the main point to be considered here is, that the period when painted glass began to be used in Europe was that which saw the triumph of the pointed over the round arch ; and it is worthy of note that the leading archæologists of France, who regard the Abbot Suger as the father of the French style of Gothic architecture, regard him also as the founder of their school of glass-painting.

Although the Germans and Flemings appear to have been in the field before the French, the last named soon took the lead in the art ; and it is probable that our earliest painted windows of glass were the work of foreign painters. With so strong an infusion of the foreign element in the priesthood at the Norman Conquest, foreign painters and craftsmen would naturally flock to this country, where they would be warmly welcomed by their fellow countrymen. In time however, with the fusion of the alien with the native art, we acquired a distinctive manner, which, although it bore a general resemblance to the northern style of glass-painting, was sufficiently characteristic to entitle it to rank as an independent school.

With regard to the styles and periods of transition it may be said concerning painted glass as of architecture, that there was a continual putting off of the old fashion, and a putting on of the new.

As regards both material and colour the glass of the Early English period has never been approached, although a modern maker of stained glass will tell you that much of the gem-like colour and brilliancy of the glass of the thirteenth

I

century was due in no small measure to the uneven hue of colour arising from the irregular mixing
of the pigments with the vitreous materials in
the crucibles.   Anyone who cares to examine
closely a piece of genuine glass of this early period,
cannot fail to notice the uneven character of
the surfaces, and the smallness of the pieces
used, both indications of crudeness in production.
But the early workers, like true artists, turned the
faults in the manufacture of the raw material to
positive advantage, by deepening the hues for the
shadows and obtaining the half-tones without the
use of shading ; and the light being unequally
transmitted, produced that remarkable richness
and depth of colouring that is at once the delight
and the despair of the modern worker in coloured
glass.

As we look at a piece of ancient glass in a village
church at the present day we must bear in mind
that the great surfaces of the whitewashed walls
were in all probability covered with fresco paintings, which not only served to illustrate the gospel
history, but to lead the eye gradually to the
stronger colours of the windows.   Nowadays old
glass does not look its best in the strong reflected
glare thrown by whitewashed walls, and it requires
a certain amount of " dim religious light " to re-
veal to the full the harmonious brilliancy and
unequal display of light that is so characteristic
of our earliest specimens of coloured glass.   But

we must remember that age and incrustations play a great part in the present effect of old glass. We do not know what the glass looked like when new, any more than we know what our modern glass will look like when it is as old.

Among our best English examples of early glass is that in the choir aisles of Canterbury Cathedral, which is considered to be portions of the original glazing that was put in when this part of the building was rebuilt after a fire in 1174. The general design is composed of panels of various forms, in which are depicted subjects from the Holy Scripture, with backgrounds of deep blue or red ; the spaces between the panels are filled with mosaic patterns in which blue and red colours predominate, and the whole design is framed in an elaborate border of leaves and scroll work.

Of thirteenth century glass we have some magnificent examples — unfortunately few unmutilated—as at York, where is the five-light lancet window, situated in the north end of the transept, and known as the Five Sisters of York. Of this date, also, are the large circular window of Lincoln Cathedral, and the windows at Chetwode Church, Bucks ; Westwell, Kent ; West Horsley, Surrey ; and Becket's Crown, Canterbury.

In the fourteenth century the glass was made smoother, of a uniform thickness, more diaphanous, and the colours used were brighter ; but against these improvements in the manufacture of the raw

material we have to put the loss of that depth, tone,
and character, which gave such dis-
Fourteenth tinction to the earlier windows.
Century This period, however, saw a great
Glass. advance in the drawing of figures,
the drapery is fuller, and the style has less of the
quality which artists know as " tightness." At
the same time with more learned drawing something of the artless simplicity and devotional sen-
timent was lost. Windows of the Decorated
period continued to be arranged in panels, with the
intervening spaces filled with flowing foliage, in
which the symbolical vine and ivy leaves predominate, for symbolism made an artistic if not
a religious advance during this period. The
" smear shadow " was now introduced, although
a brown enamel was still the only pigment used,
with the exception of a yellow transparent stain
which, on firing, penetrated into the glass, and
modified or changed its colour, the original
tints being obtained in the actual manufacture
of the glass.   Single figures are more common
than in the previous style, and they are generally shown standing on pedestals beneath canopies,
whence such windows are designated " canopied "
to distinguish them from the " medallion " windows of the preceding century. In the earlier
examples the figures occupy a portion only of the
window light, but in the later examples they
cover nearly the whole of the glass.

To this period belong the east window of Gloucester Cathedral, 72 feet high and 38 feet broad, and other fine windows at Tewkesbury Abbey; Merton College, Oxford; Wroxhall Abbey, Warwickshire; and the churches of Chartham, Kent; Ashchurch, Gloucester; Cranleigh, Surrey; Norbury, Derbyshire; and others. Salisbury Cathedral has retained portions, and very lovely portions, of the glazing of its west windows, enough being left to show that it was little inferior to that of the great windows of York and Gloucester. Carlisle Cathedral, too, has preserved fragments of the original glass in the tracery of the great east window, but the lower part of the glazing is modern.

The advent of the Perpendicular period gave us the third distinctive style of glass painting, easily distinguished from its predecessors. In the Early English and Decorated periods the art grew to maturity; in the Perpendicular there were indications of over-ripeness, although this period

Glass in the Perpendicular period. showed a little falling off in intelligent drawing and mechanical dexterity. But with increased skill and larger windows came a greater passion for display. The designs became more elaborate, more pictorial, in a word, more independent of their surroundings. The artists regarded the glazing as a convenient surface on which to paint a picture, and instead of plain or diapered backgrounds, buildings and landscapes were introduced. The glass itself was bright in tint, and uniform in character, but much thinner and poorer than that used in the previous styles. Regarded as pictures the windows of this period are very harmonious and artistic, although the canopies over the figures became of exaggerated proportions, and overloaded with crockets and architectural details. The figures were more highly finished, and in many instances the "stipple" shading supplanted the "smear." The use of heraldry was common, also the employment of inscriptions on long narrow scrolls. In the larger windows the subjects were arranged so that each formed a distinct picture, and we not infrequently find the design carried across the whole window without regard to the breaks caused by the mullions. The finest example of this period we have is the great eastern window of York Minster, 75 feet high, 32 feet broad, and divided into one hundred and seventeen compartments. At the dawn of the sixteenth century the art was declining, although this period gave us the famous windows of King's College Chapel, Cambridge, *circa* 1528. There was now a return to the foreigner for windows as well as for sculpture, and we have many good examples of these imported windows. Well-known instances are those in Fairford Church, Gloucestershire ; the great east window of St. Margaret's, Westminster—a representation of the Crucifixion, sent as a present by the magistrates of Dort to Henry VII; and those imported early in the last century and afterwards set up in the Lady Chapel of Lichfield Cathedral.

The Gothic school of glass-painting succumbed before the new style of the Renaissance and what is known as the mosaic-enamel method came into use. The windows were now essentially pictures, works in which the ornamental portions were subordinate to the principal subject, and in construction no less than in style, they differ greatly from the Gothic examples. The mosaic-enamel method attained its greatest perfection in Italy, where Florence was the seat of the art, which was practised by such painters as Donatello, and Lorenzo Ghiberti. The facility for pictorial effect given by the enamel colours led to an almost entire disuse of coloured glass. It was in this method that Reynolds' famous window at New College, Oxford, was painted by Jarvis, and West's windows at Windsor by Jarvis and Forrest. The enamel colours gave the painter a comprehensive palette; but they were more or less opaque, so that the first requirement of a window—the admission of light—was neglected. The ease with which the enamel pigments could be used caused painted windows to become the fashion, with the result that they eventually became mere imitations and frequently copies of oil-paintings.

The demand for painted church windows during

the last twenty or thirty years has been prodigious, and they have been turned out of the factories by the thousand.

William Morris and Edward Burne-Jones did most valuable work in rescuing the art from the commercial element by which it was being strangled, although here again one regrets that such talented artists were content to copy the methods and styles of the old workers. Few modern church windows are an unqualified success, mainly because the designers treat them as pictures, instead of media to subdue or modify, but not to obstruct the light. Every art has its limits and conventions ; and glass painting is the most limited and conventional of them all.

The Jesse window, found occasionally in our cathedrals and churches, is, strictly speaking, a representation of the genealogy of Christ, in which the various persons forming the **The Jesse** descent, are depicted on branches or **window.** scrolls of foliage. The same idea was also wrought into a branched candlestick, called a Jesse. The subject is found on a window at Llanrhaiadr y Kinmerch (Denbighshire), and on the stone work of one of the chancel windows at Dorchester, Oxfordshire, where the sculptured figures of our Lord's ancestry, on the spreading branches, form the mullions and tracery of the window. The east window of Winchester College chapel is a late fifteenth century specimen, and a very late example occurs in the painted windows of St. George's, Hanover Square, London. A very elaborate treatment of the same subject is found in carved stone on the magnificent reredos of Christchurch Priory, Hants.

We know from contemporary records that painted windows were placed in our parish churches for the religious instruction of the congregation, so that the range of subjects for the artist was almost inexhaustible. In addition to the usual ecclesiastical symbols of the Trinity, the sacred monograms, the rite of baptism, etc., there were the Passion of the Saviour and His rise in glory, the acts and effigies of the apostles, and the sufferings of the Christian martyrs.

Chapter XIV.

The Grotesque element in Religious Art.

THE grotesque element in ecclesiastical architecture and ornament, is confined, with a few exceptions, to such details of the exterior as corbels,
tympana, and gargoyles and of the interior as
bosses, pendants, capitals, misericords, bench-
ends, etc., and in gargoyles perhaps it is most
in evidence. We do not know for what, if
any, reason, these humorous and sometimes coarse
carvings should have been so freely introduced in
buildings intended for the contemplation of the
sublime and divine. In any case we must remember
that what looks grotesque to us may have looked
far otherwise to those who fashioned this kind of
ornament. As the late Romilly Allen said : " It
cannot be supposed that the sculptor of the twelfth
century would purposely throw ridicule on such
subjects as the Last Supper, or Christ in Glory ;
and yet some of the figures in these scenes are as
archaic and barbarous to look upon as many a
South Sea idol." We also know that the early
church, by the mouths of its preachers individually,
and by the decrees of its councils collectively,
opposed this type of ornament as being frivolous and

unmeaning. The second Nicene Council, A.D. 787, declared it to be "not only puerile, but altogether foolish and impious, to attempt to fascinate the eyes of the faithful in the holy place with the figures of animals or fishes, or other such devices." In an "Apology" addressed to the Abbey of St. Thierry, in the twelfth century, St. Bernard of Clairvaux, says : " Moreover, what is the use of that ridiculous monstrosity placed in the cloisters before the eyes of the brethren when occupied with their studies, a wonderful sort of hideous beauty and beautiful deformity," and so on, concluding with these words : " For God's sake ! if people are not ashamed of the extravagance of these follies, why should they not at least regret the expense required to produce them."

Gargoyles offer a fine field for the searcher after the grotesque and from many village and town churches some hideous dragon, or **Gargoyles.** terror-inspiring serpent looks down from tower angle or nave parapet. The word is generally derived from the French *gargouille,* which, in its turn, comes from the Latin, *gurgulio,* the gullet. It occurs in a French MS. of the fourteenth century as " gargale," the name of a disease peculiar to swine which causes a gurgling sound in their throats. The function of the earliest gargoyles was utility, and they were little more than orifices with a lip to shoot the rain water well away from the walls.

With the development of mediaeval art the gargoyle was fashioned with much decorative skill, and it would be difficult to find two ancient gargoyles exactly alike.   They are rarely met with before the Early English period, when they had a considerable projection from the cornices and buttresses on which they are mostly found. Among our finest examples are those adorning many of the Oxford colleges (71 H), and there is a very beautiful set on the roof of Henry VII's Chapel at Westminster.   To show that these grotesques are also to be found in the churches of quite unimportant villages, there may be mentioned that of Theberton, Suffolk, on which there are a number of unusually large and characteristic gargoyles.   Corbels also are often very grotesque pieces of carving, as witness the set at Romsey Abbey.

Turning to the interior of an old church, cathedral, or priory, we find an occasional grotesque carving on capitals, bosses, or brackets, although more frequently on corbels, bench-ends and misericords (127).   It is rare to find a cathedral, conventual, or collegiate church without misericords *in situ*.   In the Temple Church, London, there is a complete range of grotesques on the spandrels of the arches which form the wall arcade of the round portion of the church.

Chapter XV.

Church Restoration and Preservation.

THE rapid growth of archæological interest in churches and the scientific analysis of their details, plans, and enrichments, bids fair to rob our old village sanctuaries of much of the air of mystery and romance, which, to the receptive mind, gives them the greater part of their present day charm. Learned ecclesiologists write elaborate treatises on apsidal terminations and periapsidal plans, and quarrel among themselves with regard to the chronology of insignificant details. To such an extent has this microscopic dissection been carried that if one of the mediaeval craftsmen could revisit the scene of his earthly labours he could hardly fail to come to the conclusion that for many people the churches which he and his fellows built for the glory of God, were now regarded mainly as archæological museums and architectural records.

The most unobservant lover of these ancient buildings cannot fail to notice in his travels about our homeland, that a very large proportion of our old churches have been much restored since their first erection; and the greater number of such restorations have taken place during the last sixty or seventy years.

Over the appalling mutilations by Wyatt and others which took place early in the nineteenth century we will draw a veil; but legitimate restoration, in so far as any restoration can be called legitimate, began about 1840, when it was to a certain extent based on architectural principles which did not ignore entirely the artistic claims of the earlier work. Since that time however there has been a craze for restoration, a feverish anxiety to smarten up the building by scraping and plastering, until all the beauty and charm of the old weather-worn surfaces have vanished. Bishops, clergy, wealthy patrons, and architects, have rushed at the work without appearing to realise what they were doing, with the result that the work has, speaking generally, been done with far too little reflection.

The old generation of parsons may have had their social and scholastic shortcomings, but they had the saving grace of knowing their own limitations. The hesitation they displayed in retouching or restoring any portion of the fabric of their churches may, to a large extent, be ascribed to apathy, and to their indifference as to the condition of the material structures wherein they ministered; but it is just possible that some of them loved their churches too well to experiment on the buildings with the limited amount of information at their command. We will credit them with the knowledge that the blocked-up window hid some delicate tracery, and that the covered doorway disguised some noble arch. They frankly acknowledged the difficulties of the situation and were content, for the most part, to keep the buildings in repair. Popular lectures on architecture, followed by a perfect flood of archæological text-books, have fired the imaginations of all those in charge of churches possessing hidden charms, with the result that they have come to be regarded as the legitimate playground of antiquaries, rather than as the calm and impressive Houses of God.

In many cases too the so-called restorers have swept away such things as ancient fonts, screens, and panelling. Old reading desks, beautifully carved and black with age, are replaced by glittering brass from Birmingham, and as the ancient benches were not as comfortable as sofas, they too were broken up for firewood. Not many miles from the spot where these lines are written, there is lying half-buried in the ground of a churchyard, a beautifully carved Norman font, while a hideous modern thing within the church bears an inscription from which it is obvious that it was placed there more for the gratification of Jones than for the glorification of God.

Then again, many a manor house and hall are

adorned and beautified with property that has been filched from the village church.

Who is primarily to blame for this state of things it is hard to say, but when the lady of the manor reclines on sofa cushions made from mediaeval altar cloths, and the village squire has the ancient rood-screen converted into a hall fire-place, it is surely time to protest against the acquisition of church property by private individuals.

Perhaps the most curious thing about all restoration so-called, is that when an old building is admired for its mellowness, its look of hoary antiquity, the first thing done by the restorers is to obliterate all those harmonious tints and colours with which nature endows a building only after the lapse of centuries. Walls, doors, windows, roofs, etc., are made to appear as they who do the work imagine they appeared when first erected. Mouldings are recut, carved surfaces scraped, soft edges made sharp, until every one of the very qualities that we profess to admire has been wiped away, and the building has, to use a common phrase, been " brought up-to-date." To admire a building because it looks old, yet to stand by in apathetic silence while every trace of Time is wiped off, is one of those extraordinary contra-dictions of the human mind so difficult to account for. The clerical and lay guardians of these priceless memorials of the past, must surely perceive the impossibility of attempting to restore that which is for ever lost, and the harmfulness of destroying in their own village church all evidences of its antiquity.

It must be obvious to everyone that genuine restoration would be rather in the direction of preservation pure and simple. The insertion of a quoin stone where the old one is so much worn as to unduly strain its fellows, need surely not include the scraping and cleaning of the whole tower for the purpose of making it match the one new stone, a frequent occurrence. With regard to the carved capitals and details it is always a failure to have them recut, for neither the religious environment, nor the hand of the dead craftsman can ever be recalled. Mr. Reginald Blomfield has said: "What is offensive in restoration is its sham history, the hypocrisy of affecting to reproduce the old work with such fidelity that one has to look twice before one can find the incontestable marks of the beast."

And now, having had our grumble, let it be acknowledged freely that our churches were built for divine worship and anything that makes them more convenient for this purpose cannot fail to be beneficial to the community, provided always that such additions and alterations as are regarded as essential, are frankly and honestly modern, and do not pose as imitations of mediaeval work. There have indeed been some noble and genuine restorations by Pugin, Scott, Street, and a few

K

others, while an ever increasing number of architects are ready to prove that modern additions
can be made to a church, even in the present day
when the comfort of the body is regarded as of
equal if not of greater importance than the welfare
of the soul, without obliterating the work of the
ancient builders.   Could not the word " restoration " be expunged from the architect's dictionary,
and " preservation " substituted for it ?

With regard to the building of modern churches
it is rather singular that, with a few notable exceptions, architects are content to copy the work
of their mediaeval predecessors.   For this the
architects are not wholly to blame, for the main
thing required by those who find the money for
building churches to-day, is a correct imitation,
or reproduction, of mediaeval work.   Once determine the peculiarities of the style to be imitated,
and it may be reproduced to any extent, as was
proved by the Gothic revivalists of the last century
If church architecture said its last word four hundred
years ago, which one is loth to believe, imitative
reproduction of the work of an age from which
the imitators are separated by four or five centuries of such marvellous religious and social
events as have intervened since the originals were
produced, must at its best be but a soulless thing.
The craftsmen of the Middle Ages worked up to
the full intelligence of their day, and their work
was imbued with individuality of thought as well

as with deep religious feeling. The man, who, working in the twentieth century, deliberately ignores all the national and social influences of his day, and all that distinguishes it from the mediaeval period, lays aside his individuality, and so disqualifies himself from producing anything more than a copy. The one thing wanted—perfect independence of thought—is, one fears, seldom allowed the church architect. The hope of its acceptance lies in the advent of an ecclesiastical architect of real genius, who, having studied the best productions of his predecessors, would work in their spirit without treading servilely in their footsteps.

We ought to build good churches although our architects have not the hereditary knowledge of craft or the religious inspiration of their mediaeval predecessors. Yet the fact remains that with all the gifts of science we have not so far produced a greater building than those erected not only in mediaeval, but in pre-Christian days. The money we have, the men we may have, the finest materials from the storehouses of the world lie at our door, but the time we cannot spare, and without time for patient, joyous labour, nothing can be achieved in the realms of literature, art, and architecture, that will reflect faithfully the grace, the dignity, and the force of happy life.

Men, money, science, and learning have failed to produce great buildings mainly because the rush of modern life gives no time for dignified and leisured production. Lorenzo Ghiberti laboured forty years at the bronze gates of the Baptistery at Florence, and Michael Angelo said they were worthy to be the Gates of Paradise. To the production of such a masterpiece the craftsman gave his all, his very life, and the joy of his work was the greatest of his many rewards.

DETACHED HOLY WATER STOUP
AT WOOTTON COURTNEY, SOMERSET.

Appendix A.

The Evolution of Church Plans.

ALL English Church plans—however much they may vary in detail—are based upon two types, or resolve themselves into two classes, which may be called (a) the longitudinal and (b) the cruciform. The root of the first is that of two rectangles end to end, the root of the second is the church with transepts at the junction of nave and chancel.

Plans 2, 3, 6, 7 and 8 (*see* pp. 150 and 151) show the development and varieties of the longitudinal plan. Plans 4, 5, and 9 that of the cruciform. Thus : No. 2 (disregarding the porch) is the church with nave and chancel only. No. 3, the same plan with the Norman variation of an apsidal east end. No. 6, the longitudinal church with aisles to nave only. No. 7, aisles carried to full length of nave and chancel making a perfect rectangle. No. 8, the longitudinal plan of nave and chancel with aisles, as modified by the addition of several chantry chapels as at A, B, C, D, E, F and G.

Of the cruciform plan the development is illustrated thus : Fig. 4. The simplest form (disregarding the tower), *i.e.*, nave, chancel and transepts—all without aisles. Fig. 5, the same form, but with aisles to nave and chancel, [observe both with reference to the longitudinal and the cruciform type that aisled churches may have many variations, *e.g.*, there may be one or two nave aisles, one or two chancel aisles, one or (rarely) two aisles to one or both transepts]. Fig. 9, the cruciform plan with aisles as modified by chantry chapels, as at A, B, C, D, E, F, G, H, I. Observe again that, as in the evolution of the longitudinal plan, the effect here also is to bring one again in the end to an almost perfect rectangle.

Many authorities regard the Roman basilica as the pro-

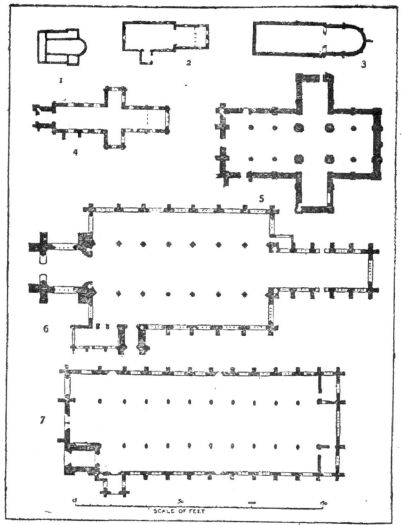

SCALE OF FEET

(1) SILCHESTER, HANTS; (2) TANGMERE, SUSSEX; (3) HADLEIGH, ESSEX;
(4) ACHURCH, NORTHANTS; (5) ST. CROSS, WINCHESTER; (6) BOSTON,
LINCS; (7) ST. NICHOLAS, KING'S LYNN.

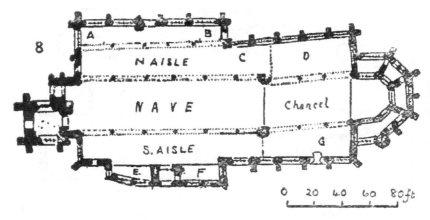

ST. MICHAEL, COVENTRY.

totype of the English churches, so a plan of the foundation
of a little basilican church recently unearthed at Silchester
is added—Fig. 1.

[We are indebted to Mr. Francis Bond, M.A., author, and to Mr. B. T.
Batsford, publisher, of *Gothic Architecture in England*, for permission to
reproduce plans 1, 2, 3, 4, 5, 6 and 7, and to Mr. A. Hamilton Thompson,
M.A., F.S.A., author, and to the Cambridge University Press, publishers,
of *The Historical Growth of the English Parish Church*, for permission to
reproduce plans 8 and 9.]

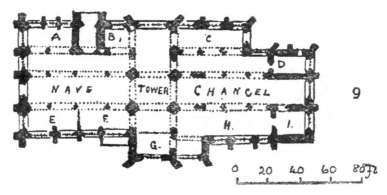

HOLY TRINITY, COVENTRY.

Appendix B.

The Isometric Plan.

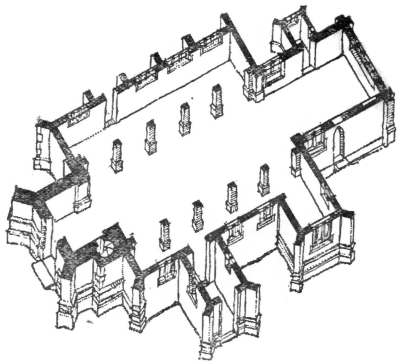

An isometric plan is a material aid to the visualisation of a church. It can be quite easily—if roughly—made. Take an ordinary ground plan, tilt it at an angle of about 45 degrees, and draw down vertical lines—all of the same length—from every corner of the ground plan. The result will be a bird's eye view of exterior and interior as it would appear if the building were sliced off at a height of some feet from the ground. The plan can be carried farther at choice by inserting lines to join the lower ends of the verticals, as in the drawing above, in which the solid black lines represent the original ground plan.

Appendix C.

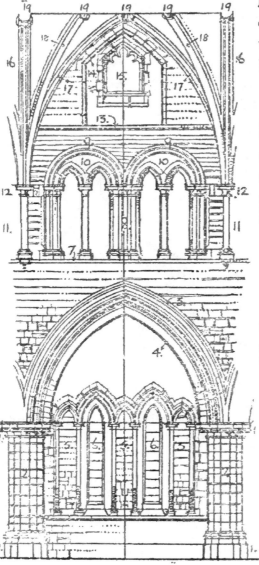

Key to Diagram of Interior Elevation of one bay of a Church

Clerestory—

19   Bosses.
18   Vaulting Rib (Intermediate).
17   Vaulting Rib (Diagonal).
16   Vaulting Rib (Transverse).
15   Clerestory Window.
14   ,,   Arch.
13   ,,   String Mould.

Blind Storey or Triforium—

12   Capital of Vaulting Shaft.
11   Vaulting Shaft.
10   Triforium Arches.
9   Triforium Arches.
8   Pier of Triforium.
7   Triforium String.

Ground Storey—

6   Aisle Windows.
5   ,,   Wall Arcading.
4   Arches of Nave Arcade.
3   Hood Mould.
2   Nave Piers.
1   Capitals and Bases of Nave Piers.

Appendix D.

The Evolution of Mouldings.

MOULDINGS are quite the most important feature of the ornamentation of architectural members, and as they are the most difficult to define in such a way that the definition shall carry with it a real description of the thing defined, a page of illustrations is attached.

If a stone or block of timber be cut in such a way that the various faces (155-A) meet in a right angle on each edge (155-B) it is said to be squared, and the edges are said to be square-edged (155-1). If the evenness of the square-edge has been broken by accident, and the workman to hide the fault slices down the edge in a regular slice cut at an angle of about 45 degrees, it is then said to be chamfered the new face being called a chamfer (155-2), especially if it be carried right through the whole length or height of the stone or timber. If however it be not carried right through, the workman does not usually stop the chamfer suddenly or abruptly, but cuts from the square-edge into the chamfer, or leads from the chamfer to the square-edge in various ways more or less ornamental or simple. Such a chamfer is said to be a stop or stopped chamfer (155-2). There are seven chamfers, the plain, the hollowed, the sunk, the swelled, the wavy, the ogee and the bracket. The plain (155-2) is cut simply across leaving a flat face diagonally placed as regards the original faces of the stone or timber. If hollowed (155-3) it is gouged out with a gouge so as to form a curved channel cut into the edge. The edges of the hollow chamfer are often themselves plain chamfered. The sunk chamfer (155-4) results from the workman cut-

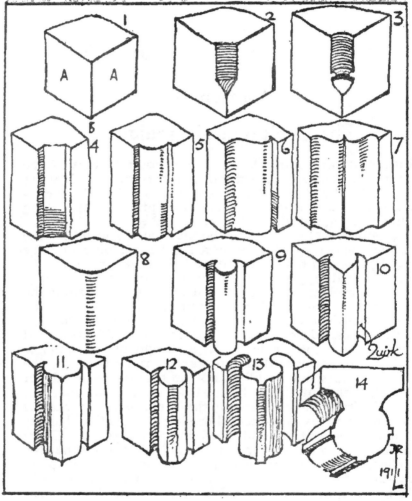

1. A—faces, B—square edge. 2. Stopped chamfer. 3. Hollow chamfer
and stop. 4. Sunk chamfer. 5. Swelled chamfer. 6. Wavy chamfer.
7. The bracket. 8. Rounded off. 9. Bowtell. 10. Pointed bowtell.
11. Pear-shaped bowtell. 12. Chamfered bowtell. 13. Filleted bowtell.
14. Roll and triple fillet.

ting at right angles into the faces at some little distance from the edge to be cut off, and then digging out the chamfer. The swelled chamfer (155-5) is formed by cutting in at right angles at first as in the last example, but rounding off the chamfer. The ogee (155-6) is a compound of the hollow and the swelled, first starting as a hollow on one side and then swelling out on the other, producing an S form on plan. This curve of double flexure, partly concave and partly convex, is termed the ogee, and came into use about 1315. The bracket (155-7) consists of two wavy mouldings side by side, the one being reversed, and so on plan resembling the printer's bracket. The wavy is the swelled chamfer worked like the bracket, but with the central pointed groove omitted.

Instead of chamfering the edge another plan is to round it off (155-8), but a simple rounding off looks so weak and characterless and undefined and undecided, that the mason more often cuts a quirk (155-10) down each face of the stone or timber, as in sinking a sunk chamfer, and by continuing the rounding off process the edge becomes a bead or attenuated shaft, like a stick or the shaft of an arrow or lance, and from this last resemblance it was called in the Middle Ages a boltell or bowtell, *i.e.* a small bolt. But it is more often called the roll moulding (155-9).

In Early Norman, if we did not know that the arches with their various orders were built to support a wall we should imagine that they had been cut through a pre-existing wall, and the edges left square between the face of the arch and its inner or under-side or soffit. Then the edges were cut into a roll, which roll followed the contour of the arch, up one side and down the other. Then the quirk gradually got deeper and deeper, the roll or bowtell itself standing out pear-shaped on plan (155-10). Sometimes the original edge was left, but sometimes the workman cut shallow hollows on either side of the edge, and so he got the pointed bowtell (155-11). Then the edge was chamfered (155-12), and a little quirk cut on

Mouldings.

each side leaving a square-edged fillet standing on the roll, which is then said to be filleted (155-13). Later the roll sometimes bears two or even three fillets, the roll and double fillet, or the roll and triple fillet (155-14), as it is then called, as the case may be.

Although mouldings had long been used on capitals and bases, on cornices, and so on, the moulding of arches and jambs in the Middle Ages, but particularly of arches, had a distinct growth and development all its own, as thus indic ted, and the various groupings of the different kinds of cLamfers, and the projections and hollows and quirks arising from either chamfering or rounding off, result in those marvellous and intricate effects of light and shade running up jambs and other uprights, around the sides of the arches, and along horizontal courses, or projecting strings or along the timbers of roofs, and screens, and in fact everywhere where mouldings could be employed. At first, in Gothic, they were deep in hollows and so corresponding projections were left (Early English period), then they became close and compact (Decorated period), and lastly flat and shallow (Perpendicular period). This follows the growth of scientific masonry. At first walls and piers were thick, heavy and massive, and the mouldings could be multitudinous and deep. Then walls being better constructed they became thinner ; lastly, masonry became so perfect that stone was economised and there was no room for deep and multitudinous mouldings. Architecture was not debased, but masonry had attained perfection.

Appendix E.

A Short Bibliography of English Ecclesiastical Architecture.

Adeline, J.	Art Dictionary of Terms.
Bishop, Rev. H. H.	Architecture in relation to our Parish Churches.
Bland, W.	Arches, Piers, Buttresses, etc.
Blomfield, R.	Short History of Renaissance Architecture.
Bloxam, M. H.	Principles of Gothic Architecture.
Bond, Francis	Gothic Architecture in England.
,, ,, [see p. 206]	Fonts and Font Covers.
,, ,,	Misericords in English Churches.
,, ,,	Screens and Galleries in English Churches.
,, ,,	Stalls and Tabernacle Work in English Churches.
Bond, F. Bligh, and Dom Bede Camm.	Rood Screens and Rood Lofts.
Brandon, R. & J. A.	Parish Churches.
Brown, G. Baldwin	The Arts in Early England.
Carter, J.	The Ancient Architecture of England
Colling, J. K.	Details of Gothic Architecture.
Corroyer, E.	Gothic Architecture.
Cox, J.C. & Harvey,A.	English Church Furniture.
Cram, R. Adams	Church Building.
,, ,,	English Parish Churches.
Davidson, E. A.	Gothic Stonework.
Ecclesiological (late Cambridge Camden) Society, The.	A Handbook of English Ecclesiology.

Eden, C. H.	Black Tournai Fonts in England.
Fergusson, J.	Handbook of Architecture.
,, ,,	History of Architecture.
Fletcher, Banister	A History of Architecture.
Garbett, E. L.	Principles of Design in Architecture.
Macklin, H. W.	The Brasses of England.
Markland, J. H.	Remarks on Churches.
Moore, C. H.	Development and Character of Gothic Architecture.
Paley, F. A.	Manual of Gothic Architecture.
,, ,,	Manual of Gothic Mouldings.
Parker, J. H.	A.B.C. of Gothic Architecture.
,, ,,	Concise Glossary of Architecture.
,, ,,	Introduction to the Study of Gothic Architecture.
Perkins, Rev. T.	Handbook of Gothic Architecture.
Prior, Ed. S.	History of Gothic Art.
Pugin, A.	Examples of Gothic Architecture.
,, ,,	Specimens of Gothic Architecture.
Raven, J. J.	The Bells of England.
Rickman, Thos.	Gothic Architecture.
,, ,,	Attempts to discriminate the styles of Architecture in England.
Ruskin, John	Stones of Venice.
Scott, G.	History of Church Architecture.
Sharpe, Edmund	The Seven Periods of English Architecture
,, ,,	Treatise on the Rise and Progress of Window Tracery.
Thompson, A. H.	The Ground Plan of the English Parish Church.
,, ,,	The Historical Growth of the English Parish Church.
Wall, J. C.	Shrines of British Saints.

This bibliography does not claim to be complete, but is a useful selection of books on various phases of the subject which may be studied for further information.

Appendix F.

A Glossary of some of the Principal Terms used in Ecclesiastical Architecture.

Abacus. Derived from the Greek Abax—a tray or flat board. The slab forming the upper part of the capital of a column, pier, etc. (48).

Abbey. A monastery governed by an abbot (*see* Collegiate Church, Monastery, Priory).

Abutment. The wall, pier or buttress from which an arch, roof or vault springs, or by which their thrust is met.

Acanthus. A plant, the leaves of which are represented in the capitals of the Corinthian order (*see* Order) and in classical ornament generally.

Aisle. French *Aile*, a wing, the lateral division of a church.

Almery, Aumbrey, or Aumery. A recess or small cupboard in the wall of a church, used to contain the chalices, patens, etc. It is sometimes near the piscina, but more usually on the north side of the chancel. Practically it formerly did duty as the safe of the church.

Altar. A table-like or tomb-like construction, usually of stone, used for the administration of the sacrament of the Eucharist.

Ambulatory. A sheltered place for exercise in walking; a cloister; a gallery; a processional aisle round the back of the High Altar.

Angle. There are two aspects of the angle, (1) in the case of a projection, *e.g.* a buttress, the external one, solid, a salient, quoin, arris or edge, (2) the reverse or interior aspect, in which case it is known as a re-entering or recessed angle or nook. A shaft placed on the former is called an angle-shaft, but where as in doorways it is placed as it were in a nook, it is termed a nookshaft (45).

Ante-Chapel. A transept or the bay or bays ritually west of the chapel proper, especially of a college.

Apse. A semi-circular or polygonal extension at the eastern end of the choir or aisles.

Arcade (*see* **Colonnade**). A series of arches, open, or closed with masonry, and supported by piers, columns or pillars (17, 20) (*see* Pier-Arcade, Triforium, Wall-Arcade).

Arch. A construction of wedge-shaped bricks or stones so placed as by mutual pressure to support each other and a superincumbent weight (52).

Architecture. The art and science of designing and constructing buildings on correct and scientific principles. The manner in which buildings are designed and constructed. Architecture is chiefly Classical, *i.e.* Greek or Roman; or Gothic, *i.e.* of mediaeval times, these two practically embodying the principles of all other architecture, ancient or modern (*see* Classic, Gothic. Renaissance).

Architrave. (a) In Classical architecture the lowest division of the entablature resting immediately on the abacus of the capital; (b) the ornamental mouldings round the openings of doors, windows, etc.

Archivolt (*see* **Soffit**). The moulding carried round the arch-stones or voussoirs of an arch, corresponding to the architrave. Also sometimes applied to the soffit or under and inner surface of the curve of an arch, from impost to impost.

L

Arcuated. Arched.

Ashlar. Shaped or squared stones used in building, as distinguished from those in the rough or rubble (q.v.)

Astragal. (1) A small semi-circular bead or moulding. (2) The necking of a capital just above the shaft.

Attic-base. The base of a column, consisting of an upper and lower torus, a scotia, and fillets between them, in Classic architecture and carried on traditionally in Romanesque and Gothic.

From c. 1150—c. 1190 the lower torus was considerably flattened, and hence the base was called " the base with flattened lower roll." From c. 1190 to c. 1260 this torus became semicircular again. During the whole period, c. 1150—c. 1260, the scotia was so hollowed out, as to be capable of holding water. From c. 1240 to c. 1350 the scotia was omitted, and the base is said to be with double or triple roll as the case may be (*see* Water-holding-base).

Ball-Flower. An ornament, placed in a hollow moulding and resembling a ball in the cup of a flower with enclosing petals, (71) to be found in late Norman work, but especially in work of the first half of the fourteenth century, and sometimes earlier, sometimes later. It occurs in the greatest profusion in Gloucestershire and Herefordshire (*see* Moulding).

Base. The lower member of a column, pier or wall (*see* Attic-base, and Water-holding-base).

Basilica. A Roman law-court. Originally an open court surrounded by covered colonnades. Later, the open court being covered in by a roof carried on walls built up upon the entablature of the colonnades, such walls being pierced with windows, and forming a clerestory, the whole became a vast hall or nave with aisles.

Batter. The slope of a wall that is not built with a perpendicular outer face, thus built to withstand some thrust.

Glossary. 163

Battlement. An embattled parapet : a parapet having a series of indentations, originally a military device but used on churches as an ornament. In later work miniature battlements were added to the transoms of windows, the abacus, the top rails of screens and elsewhere. The solid rising parts are termed merlons, the openings or interstices between the merlons are termed embrasures.

Bay. A compartment of a church consisting of a section of each storey and marked off by the piers of the arcade, the buttresses, or other features which are repeated in the construction of nave, chancel or transepts. (153).

Bead. A narrow rounded moulding, a small torus or bowtell (*see* Moulding).

Beak Head. An ornament of Norman workmanship consisting of grotesque bird or animal-like heads placed in the hollows of mouldings with the beaks or tongues encircling the round (44 B).

Billet. An ornament much used in Norman work and formed by cutting notches in a moulding, so that the remaining parts resembled wooden billets (44 E).

Blind Storey. A blank wall below the clerestory where otherwise the triforum is ranged (153).

Boss. A projecting mass generally carved. Bosses, usually of foliage or grotesques, are placed at the intersection of the ribs of vaults and ceilings and at the ends of hood mouldings.

Bowtell. A plain round moulding ; the torus. (155).

Braces. Inclined timbers used in partitions and roofs which brace or tie together the main timbers. As these timbers at the same time serve to support and stiffen the framing as well as to keep timbers from sagging, they are also termed struts. (80).

Broach Spire. An octagonal spire standing on, cutting

Broach Spire—*continued.*

into, and springing from the square pyramidal top of a tower, generally without a parapet. The corner of the square pyramid which rises against and dies into each diagonal face of the octagonal spire is termed the broach. Originally the term broach designated the whole spire. (119 *a* and *b*).

Buttress. A projection from the wall, giving it additional strength to resist the thrusts of arches, roof or vaults. (53)

Canopy. (1) Strictly a tester of stone, wood, metal or stuff over an altar, seat or tomb, and generally any covering.

(2) An ornamental hood or projection representing the front of a canopy over doors, windows, niches, tombs, sedilia, piscinas, etc., and rarely found except in Decorated and Perpendicular work (*see* Tabernacle-work). (90).

Capital. The head of a column, pillar, or pilaster, found in a great variety of shapes (44, 48, 61, etc.), either moulded, or partly moulded, partly carved. The main body of the capital between the abacus and the astragal is called the bell. (*See* Acanthus, Volute.)

Cathedral. The principal church of a diocese in which is the official seat or throne of the bishop.

Chamfer. The narrow longitudinal surface formed by cutting away, at an angle or bevel of about 45 degrees, the rectangular edge of wood or stone work. (155)

Chancel. The choir or eastern part of a church, appropriated to the use of those who officiate in the performance of the services and often screened from the nave.

Chantry-Chapel. An endowed chapel often containing the tomb of the founder, and in which masses were said, the endowment for the chanting or saying of which is the chantry. The term chantry is often incorrectly applied to the chapel itself. (155).

Chapel. (1) A church in a parish, which is not the parish church, but which is either served by the parish clergy, or attached to some house or institution and served by a chaplain.

(2) A small building attached to cathedrals and large churches.

(3) Any part of a church having its own altar and often screened off.

Chapter-House. The council chamber in which the abbot, prior and brethren of a monastic body or the dean and chapter of a cathedral church meet for the transaction of business.

Chevet. A series of chapels round the east end of a continental church or church, such as Westminster Abbey, built under continental influence.

Chevron. An ornament characteristic of the late Norman period and divided into several equal portions chevron-wise or zig-zag (44).

Choir. Properly that part of the church only containing the stalls for the singing or saying of the choir-offices by the choir of monks or canons in a greater church. When these stalls are eastward of the crossing and wholly contained in the eastern limb that limb itself is termed the choir, and is therefore the constructional choir. When the choir enclosed with screens is placed in the crossing or in the eastern bays of the nave the choir is then termed the ritual choir.

Church. It is convenient to classify churches either as " greater " or " lesser." The " greater " churches include cathedral, abbey or monastic and collegiate churches ; the " lesser," the parish and other small churches or chapels. It should be noted, however, that these terms relate to the relative importance and not necessarily or always, to the size.

Cinquefoil. *See* Foil.

Classic. *See* Architecture, Column, Entablature, Entasis, Gothic, Order, Pediment, Pilaster, Renaissance.

Clear-Story or Clerestory. An upper storey standing above or clear of the adjacent roofs, and pierced by windows (153).

Cloister. A covered walk or ambulatory generally forming part of a quadrangle in cathedral or college or elsewhere

Clustered Column. Several columns or shafts in a cluster carrying one load.

Collegiate Church. A church ministered to by a body of priests formed into a corporation or collegium. The priests were called secular canons ; distinguished from the regular priests inasmuch as they did not live according to monastic rule but each one resided in his own house.

Colonnade (*see* **Arcade**). A row or rows of columns supporting an entablature.

Column. A vertical support in classical architecture, consisting of base, shaft and capital, and conforming to the rules of the orders. *See* Order, Pier, Pillar.

Conoid. In vaulting the half or quarter cone formed by the branching out of each group of ribs from the spring to the ceiling (*see* Fan-Vaulting, Pendentive, 2).

Coping. The top course of a parapet or wall where exposed, frequently sloping to throw off rain water. When the upper surface is sloped in one direction it is termed feather-edged, when sloped in opposite directions, saddle-backed.

Corbel. Usually a moulded or carved ornament projecting from the walls, acting as a bracket and capable of bearing a superincumbent weight that is not intended to rest upon or in the wall itself. (33).

Corbel Table. A series of small arches or lintels at the top of a wall, resting on corbels and supporting a cornice battlement or parapet (17. 33) (*see* Table).

Cornice. The horizontal moulded projecting top, as of a pedestal, pier, door, window, wall or room.

Course. A horizontal line of stones or bricks in the wall of a building.

Credence. A table or shelf on which the elements of the Eucharist are placed before consecration. In the form of a shelf it is sometimes found at the back of the niche of the piscina (q.v.)

Cresting. Ornament arising above the top of a parapet or screen.

Crockets. Projecting ornaments in the form of leaves, flowers, etc., used to embellish the angles of pinnacles, spires, gables, canopies, etc. (60, 71).

Cross. The accepted symbol of the Christian religion and an architectural church ornament usually placed upon the apex of the gable.

Crossing. In cruciform churches, the part of the building where the nave, transepts and chancel meet. (150-5).

Cruciform. In the form of a cross.

Crypt. Sometimes called the undercroft. A vaulted chamber, usually underground and in churches, generally under the east end. (126).

Cupola. A ceiling or roof, concave internally, convex externally. A semi-sphere. A large cupola is termed a dome (q.v.) In late Gothic spirelets of pinnacles and turrets were often replaced by ogee-shaped (*see* Ogee) cupolas.

Cusps. Projecting points giving the foliated appearance to tracery, arches, panels, etc. (*see* Foil). (75).

Diaper Work. Small patterns carved in low relief repeated in squares, lozenges and other geometrical forms and closely covering wall surfaces.

Dog Tooth. *See* Tooth Ornament.

Dome. A large cupola or hemispherical roof, vault or ceiling, often surmounted by a lantern (q.v.) The Gothic version of a dome is to be seen in the octagon or crossing at Ely Cathedral, and this is surmounted by a large octagonal lantern.

Dormer. A window pierced through a sloping roof. (119).

Dripstone. A projecting ledge or narrow moulding over the heads of doorways, windows, etc., externally, to carry off the rain. Where square-shaped in late Gothic it is known as a Label. Used internally it is termed a Hood-Mould. (45, 74).

Drop Arch. One whose centres are on the line of, and between the points of, springing (55).

Elevation. A drawing to scale (*i.e.* not in perspective) of the face or vertical parts of a building (153). *See* Plan, Section.

Embrasure. The opening or interstice between the merlons of an embattled parapet (*see* Parapet).

Entablature. In Classical architecture the horizontal superstructure supported by a series of columns.

Entasis. A slight outward curve on a spire or the shaft of a column, or upward curve of the horizontal lines of buildings intended to correct the optical impression of hollowness arising from straight lines.

Fan-Tracery. Tracery formed by the ribs in vaulting, in which the ribs of each conoid or pendentive spread out equally and diverge with an equal curve in each direction, producing a fan-like appearance (Peculiar to the Perpendicular work p. 77). *See* Conoid, Pendentive, 2.

Feretory. (1) The portable bier, coffin, or shrine containing the relics of a saint.

(2) That part of a church where the shrine rested when not carried in procession (*see* Shrine).

Fillet. A flat projecting band frequently seen on the face or sides of rounded mouldings and sometimes between mouldings. It is often that part of the original face of the stone left unmoulded (*see* Roll Moulding). (169).

Finial. The carved top, in the form of conventional flowers, which terminates a bench end, pinnacle or canopy. (76 B)

Flamboyant. Curvilinear tracery, whereof the panels assume flame-like waves and ungeometrical and irregular shapes. A continental form of advanced Curvilinear work contemporary with the Rectilinear work of this country.

Floriated. Flowered, carved with flowers.

Flying Buttress. A buttress in the form of a semi-arch, usually transferring the thrust of the main roof from the clerestory walls to the main or aisle buttresses. (82).

Foil. A lobe between cusps in tracery. An opening is foiled when it is broken into three, four or five leaf-shaped lobes by cusps (q.v.) becoming a trefoil, quatrefoil. or cinquefoil (*see* Foliation).

Foliaged. Leaved, carved with leaves, foliage.

Foliation. An arch, circle or other opening with an inner foiled or cusped order is foliated. (66).

Font. The stone tank, basin, or vessel for holding the consecrated water used in baptism. (106).

Four-leaved Flower. A characteristic ornament especially of the later Gothic period, consisting of four leaves arranged in a conventional form (square) in the hollows of mouldings. (76).

Fresco. Paintings executed on wall plaster before it has dried.

Frith Stool. A seat placed in the most sacred portion of a church, the resort of those claiming the right of sanctuary.

Gable. The upper triangular part of an end wall or the

Gable—*continued.*
part of a wall at the end of a roof, carried up in front and masking the end of the roof. In Classical architecture it is termed the pediment (q.v.)

Gablet. A small gable. The roof-like termination of a buttress, or pinnacle, or niche.

Galilee. The name applied to a large porch or vestibule at the entrance of some of the greater churches.

Gargoyle. A projecting spout usually grotesquely carved and used to throw the water from the roof well away from the building. (71 H).

Gothic. The name, or rather nick-name, given in the seventeenth century to that development of early Christian Roman basilican architecture which flourished in Northern and Western Europe during the Middle Ages and up to the beginning of the seventeenth century.

Groin. The line of intersection in vaulted roofs without ribs. (77 C).

Hagioscope. *See* Squint.

Hammer-beam Roof. A form of timber roof peculiar to late Gothic work, and avoiding the use of a tie-beam from wall to wall, the thrust being taken by two brackets, the upper and horizontal member of which is the hammer-beam. (80).

Hood-Mould. An interior dripstone.

Impost. Horizontal mouldings capping a column or pier, from which the arch springs.

Intrados. *See* Soffit.

Jamb. The side of a window opening or doorway.

Jesse. An illustration, in the form of a tree growing out of the body of a figure of Jesse, of the genealogy of

Jesse—*continued.*

Christ, more generally in glass as a window, but sometimes in stone or needlework. The subject is also illustrated by means of a branched candlestick. The principal personages forming the genealogy are depicted on the various branches and culminate in the Blessed Virgin and Christ crucified.

Jube. *See* Pulpitum.

Keel. A form of bowtell moulding with the original edge left, so that on section it is pointed like the section of a boat. (155-10).

Keystone. The central stone at the top of an arch. The bosses in vaulted ceilings are frequently called keys.

King Post Roof. One in which each truss or supporting member has a central vertical post (*see* Queen Post Roof, Truss). (80 C).

Label. A square-shaped dripstone (q.v.), common in late work.

Lady Chapel. A chapel dedicated to the Blessed Virgin Mary, called " Our Lady," usually to be found in greater churches at the extreme east end of the choir or east of the north transept.

Lancet. The name used for the plain and narrow pointed windows of the Early English period (61).

Lantern. A small structure or erection, usually octagonal, surmounting a dome or tower, to admit light.

Lantern-tower. The central tower over the crossing in larger churches, the lower storey of which admits light to the crossing. At Westminster and Beverley the lantern has never been carried higher than this storey.

Lierne. A vaulting rib that is not a ridge rib or does not rise from the impost or vaulting shaft, but which distributes the thrusts between those that do, and strengthens the network of ribs.

Light. The lower and principal glazed panels of a window divided by mullions (*see* Tracery), called " day " in old writers.

Lintel. The stone or timber spanning a square-headed door or window and supporting the wall above.

Long-and-Short Work. Quoins placed alternately horizontal and vertical. Characteristic of Saxon masonry. (33 in porch).

Low Side Window. An opening usually in the south wall of the chancel low down allowing of communication between the priest and a person outside the church.

Lozenge. A name given in modern times to a Norman ornament of lozenge shape. (44 C)

Lych-Gate. From the Anglo-Saxon *Lich* a corpse. A covered gate at the entrance to a churchyard, under which mourners rested with the corpse while awaiting the clergy.

Merlon. The solid part of an embattled parapet between the openings or embrasures (*see* Battlement).

Minster. The church, usually of a monastery, whether abbey or priory, or one to which such has been an appendant. York and Beverley, however are wrongly called Minsters, as they were secular churches (*see* Collegiate Church, Abbey, Priory).

Misericord. The hinged seat of a stall having a small projecting bracket, often carved on the underside. (127)

Monastery. The collection of buildings inhabited by a brotherhood of monks.

Monastic Church. *See* Minster.

Moulding or Molding. The long channels or projections in the form of curves, hollows or angles, which adorn the edges of arches, doors, windows, bases and capitals, etc. (*see* Appendix D).

Mullions. The dividing uprights of stone or wood between the lights of windows, or the openings of screens. Sometimes also called Monials (*see* Light).

Narthex. An enclosed area or porch at the entrance to early and continental churches.

Nave. The main body of a church west of the chancel.

Necking. The bottom moulding or member of a capital (*see* Astragal, Capital).

Niche. An alcove or recess in a wall or pier for holding a statue or ornament.

Ogee. A double curve or curve of contra-flexure, somewhat like the letter S flattened or drawn out, part being concave and part convex. It answers to the Cyma or Sima reversa in Classical architecture.

Order. In Gothic architecture orders are the receding members or rings of an arch, whether moulded or not. In Classical architecture, an entire composition consisting of column (base, or pedestal and base, shaft and capital) and entablature. There are three Greek orders, Doric, Ionic and Corinthian, which the Romans increased to five by modifying the Doric and combining the Ionic and Corinthian. The former is called the Tuscan, and the latter the Composite, from its being composed of the two combined orders. The principal distinguishing feature of each is the capital. The Ionic has the volute: the Corinthian, the leaves of the acanthus: and the Composite has both.

Parapet. A dwarf wall rising above the roof level. It may be either continuous, battlemented, or pierced (*see* Battlements, Embrasure, Merlon.)

Parclose. The screen or railings dividing chancel from chancel aisle or protecting a monument or chantry chapel.

Parvise. An open space or porch at the entrance to a church, often wrongly applied to the room over a church porch.

Pediment. The low triangular wall (tympanum) with its raking cornice masking the end of the roof in Classical architecture (*see* Gable, Tympanum).

Pendant. Conoids which hang or depend from a fan-vaulted ceiling, sometimes thoroughly constructional and not merely ornamental. Also the timbers of a roof or tabernacle work continued downwards and ornamented.

Pendentive. (1) In Classic architecture, the Romans made use of domes and semi-domes, both over circular and rectangular buildings. When a dome surmounts a rectangular building, that portion of the dome which descends into each corner is called the pendentive.

(2) In Gothic architecture the squinch (q.v.) or a series of squinches would take the place of the Classic pendentive, while its own pendentive is exactly the reverse, being convex instead of concave, and forms a conoid (q.v.) (*see* also Fan-Vaulting, Pendant).

Penthouse. A covering projecting over a door, window, etc., as a protection from the weather.

Pier. The masses or clusters of masonry between doors, windows, etc. ; the supports other than columns or pillars from which arches spring. (65, 69, 81).

Pier Arcade. A series of arches opening into the aisles from the main body of a church. (20).

Pilaster. A shallow perpendicular square-edged projection from a wall, and corresponding to the column, in depth about one sixth of its width.

Pilaster-strips. Shallow projections in Norman masonry derived from the pilaster in Classical architecture. By increasing the projection it eventually developed into the buttress (q.v.)

Pillar. A term frequently confounded with column, (q.v) but the pillar differs from the column, in not being subservient to the rules of Classical architecture, and in not of necessity consisting of a single circular shaft.

Pinnacle. A small turreted ornament usually tapering towards the top, and used as a termination to, and to weight buttresses or other parts of Gothic buildings (*see* Gablet, Spirelet, Turret).

Piscina. The stone basin or sink near an altar used for cleansing the communion vessels, usually placed within a niche, but sometimes partly projecting from the face of the wall.

Plan. The representation of a building in horizontal section (*see* Elevation, Section). (150, 151).

Plinth. The lower division of the base of a column, pier or wall.

Poppy-Head. A floral ornament boldly carved on the tops of bench ends, etc.

Porch. The attached building protecting a doorway. Church porches are sometimes of two storeys the upper one containing a room or rooms. (21, 82).

Predella. The foot pace or raised platform in front of an altar, or upon which the altar stands.

Presbytery. A term sometimes used to include the whole of the choir, but more often meant to refer to the space between the eastern end of the stalls and the sanctuary.

Priory. A monastery governed by a prior, usually subordinate to an abbey.

Pulpit. An enclosed platform or stage for the delivery of sermons, and the reading of scripture, and of notices.

Pulpitum. In the greater churches the pulpitum was a second screen with a loft beyond the rood-screen or loft towards the east, and enclosing the choir on the west. The doorway into the choir was placed in its

Pulpitum—*continued.*

centre, while the space between the pulpitum and the rood screen or loft (q.v.) was entered by two doorways set in rood screen.

Quarries or Quarrels. The small diamond, square or other shaped panes used in plain glazing.

Quatrefoil. A panel or perforation with four lobes. *See* Foil.

Queen Post Roof. One in which each truss or supporting member has two vertical posts (*see* Truss, Hammer-beam Roof).

Quirk. An acute angled hollow much used between mouldings. (155).

Quoin. The external angle stones of a building, generally of ashlar.

Re-entering Angle. A right-angled recess cut in the angle (q.v.) of a wall, etc., resulting in three angles, two salients or quoins, with the re-entering angle between them.

Refectory. The dining-hall of a monastery, usually placed on the side of the cloister furthest from the nave of the church, either with its axis parallel with that of both the nave and the side of the cloister it adjoins, or else set at right angles to the axes of both of them. A feature of the interior is sometimes the pulpit for the reader.

Renaissance. The re-introduction or re-birth of the Classic in architecture at the beginning of the sixteenth century.

Reredos. The wall or screen at the back of an altar, often enriched with carving, niches, statues, etc.

Respond. The half pier or pillar supporting the end of an arcade. It is the pier fashioned to respond to or correspond with the pillar supporting the other half of the arch.

Ribs. The projecting, intersecting arches and supporting members of a vault. (77).

Rood. Originally in its Anglo-Saxon sense, a rod, stick, post, gibbet, but in its later and mediæval sense the crucifix, *i.e.* the cross with the figure of the Christ crucified.

Rood-Beam, Rood-Loft, Rood-Screen. The beam which supported the rood is called the Rood-Beam. If the Rood-Beam be part of the chancel or other screen, that screen is then called the Rood-Screen, and if this supports a loft or gallery, this latter is called the Rood-Loft (*see* Pulpitum).

Roll Moulding. The roll moulding is a large rounded projecting moulding, a torus or bowtell. Sometimes it bears one, two, or even three fillets. Often confused with the scroll moulding (q.v.) (155).

Rose Window (*see* **Wheel Window**). A term often used to denote a circular window of several lights. Sometimes called a marigold window.

Rotunda. A term used to describe a church or other building which is of circular formation both within and without.

Rubble. Walling constructed of rough stones.

Sacristy. A room used for storing the plate and valuables of the church.

Saddle-back. (1) A tower roof having gables on two sides and eaves or parapets on the others, like the span-roof of a church or other building.

(2) ·The stone roof-like terminations of a buttress or pinnacle. *See* Coping.

Sanctuary. The eastern portion of a church in which the High Altar was placed.

Scotia. The hollow dividing two rolls or mouldings, as in the Attic Base (q.v.)

M

Screen. A partition of stone or wood separating one part of a church from another. (102).

Scroll Moulding. A roll moulding in which the upper surface projects beyond the lower. (102).

Section. A drawing representing a building cut through, or with the end wall removed so as to show the interior divisions and arrangements ; or (*b*) showing the end of a member or its outline if cut through.

Sedilia. A seat or seats, generally canopied and situated on the south side of the sanctuary and used in pre-Reformation days by the officiating clergy during the pauses in the Mass. (90).

Severy. A compartment, division or bay of a building or vault.

Shaft. (1) The part of a column or pillar between the capital and the base.

(2) A slender pillar with base, shaft and capital, especially in clustered piers, in the recesses of doorways, supporting vaulting, etc.

Shrine. Often called the feretory. The coffin-case or receptacle, portable or otherwise, in which relics were deposited.

Soffit. The word means literally a ceiling, but is generally used to describe the flat under-surface of arches, cornices, stairways, etc.

Solar. A loft, or upper chamber. Sometimes applied to the rood-loft.

Spandrels. The triangular spaces of wall between an arch and the rectangular mouldings beside and over it.

Spire. The acutely pointed termination of towers, etc. Spires are either pathless, *i.e.* without any parapets (*see* Broach Spire) ; or parapetted, *i.e.* rising within a parapet and with a gutter or path around the base.

Spirelet. The spire-like termination of pendants, and small buttresses in tabernacle work, and of pinnacles and turrets.

Splay. The slanting or bevelled sloped surface of a window or other opening in the thickness of the wall. (49).

Springer. The lowest stone of an arch. *See* Voussoir.

Squinch. An arch built across the angles of a tower to take one of the diagonal sides of an octagonal spire.

Squint. An oblique opening or slit in a wall or pier for the purpose of enabling persons in the aisles or transepts to see the elevation of the Host at the High Altar. They are mostly found on the sides of the chancel arch and are frequently called hagioscopes.

Stilted Arch. One that springs, or starts its curve, at some distance above the capital or impost moulding. (52).

Stoup. A vessel for blessed water, at or near the entrance to a church.

String or String Course. A horizontal projecting band of stone in the wall of a building, usually under windows and parapets. The abacus of a capital, of an impost, or the dripstone of a window are frequently continued as strings. (52).

Struts. *See* Braces.

Tabernacle Work. A projecting canopy, or series of canopies, carried up into gablets, pinnacles and spirelets with much carved ornament, such as pendants, over stalls, niches, etc.

Table. A horizontal member in Gothic architecture. The term is generally used in conjunction with another, as corbel-table (q.v.), to denote its situation.

Tie-beam. A beam in a roof truss (q.v.) that extends from wall to wall.

Tooth Ornament. An ornament used almost exclusively in Early English, resembling a square four-leaved flower, and thought to be based on the dog-tooth violet.

Tracery. The ornamental stonework in the upper part of a window ; when formed by the branching of the mullions it is called bar-tracery and when the spandrel is pierced, plate-tracery (58). Also used largely on tombs, screens, doorways, etc.

Transepts. The projecting arms of a cruciform church, often wrongly called "cross-aisles." In the greater churches, sometimes, transepts are also found at the western end of the nave and sometimes at the eastern end of the choir.

Transition. In general a term used to describe the process of change from one style of architecture to another. In particular the transition from the Romanesque and Norman to the Early English Gothic. *C.* 1140-1190.

Transom. A horizontal bar in a panel or window.

Trefoil. A panel or perforation with three lobes. *See* Foil.

Triforium. An arcade, pierced or blank, immediately above the pier arcade. (153)

Triforium Chamber. The space under the roof of the aisle and behind the triforium.

Truss. In a roof, the inside framing of timbers repeated at regular intervals, supporting the rest of the roof. (80).

Tudor Flower. A characteristic ornament of the sixteenth century, as is implied by its name.

Tudor Arch. A four-centred arch (55).

Turret. A small tower carried up from the ground carrying a staircase, serving a larger tower or upper floor or gallery. The terminations of buttresses other than cappings or pinnacles and of the angles of towers, sometimes capped with battlements sometimes with a spirelet or cupola.

Tympanum. The space between the top of a square-headed doorway or chancel screen, or of a group of window openings, and the containing arch (45) ; in the latter case, the tympanum is sometimes pierced, producing plate-tracery (*see* Tracery 45*a*).

Under-croft. *See* Crypt.

Vault. Roofing or ceiling of stone constructed on the principal of the arch, the intersections of which are termed groins. In the pointed styles the intersections are usually ribbed, the ribs forming the supporting arches which are first built and the spaces between are afterwards closed with a " filling " of wedge-shaped stones (*see* Ribs, Fan-Vaulting). (77).

Vaulting Shafts. Small shafts sometimes rising from the floor, sometimes from the capital of a pillar and sometimes from a corbel, and intended as supports for the ribs of a vault.

Vesica Piscis. A figure formed by arcs of two equal circles cutting each other in their centres. Very commonly found on episcopal and monastic seals.

Volute. The top member of an Ionic capital beneath the abacus, resembling a roll of paper, rolled up from the two ends, with the rolls downwards and projecting at the sides and the centre depressed.

Voussoir. The wedge-shaped stones forming an arch, the top centre one of which is called the keystone and those at the impost or starting point of the curve are the springers. The parts of the arch between the springers and the keystone are called the haunches. The upper and outer surface is the Extrados, the inner and lower surface is the Intrados or Soffit (q.v.)

Wagon Roof or Wagon Vault. A semi-cylindrical roof or vault (q.v.) (77A, 80c).

Wall Arcade. Blank arcading carried along the surfaces of a wall as an ornament.   (17).

Water-holding Base. The form which the attic base took between 1150 and 1260, so called because the scotia was so amply hollowed out as to form a channel capable of holding water (60 H).

Wheel Window. A circular window with spoke-like shafts radiating from a hub-like centre and so resembling a wheel (17).   *See* Rose-Window.

Zig-zag. *See* Chevron.

Topographical Index.

(Illustrations are indicated by an asterisk).

County Index.

As the ecclesiology of various counties or groups of counties and districts [such for instance as the West of England (including Herefordshire), or East Anglia] is often peculiar to itself or otherwise characteristic, distinct references to such counties or districts are indexed separately, immediately following the name. For the further convenience of the reader all other references to individual places are also grouped here according to counties.

DORSET.

81. Beaminster, Broadwindsor, Cattistock, Corton, Dorchester, Fordington St. George, Maiden Newton, Melbury Bubb, Milton Abbas, Radipole, Sherborne, Studland, Wareham, Wimborne.

DURHAM.

Bishop Auckland, Durham, Escombe, Jarrow.

EAST ANGLIA.

52, 81, 99, 107, (Norfolk, Suffolk, Cambridge, Essex).

ESSEX.

43. Blackmore, Bradwell-on-Sea, Chelmsford, Greensted, Great Bardfield, Hadleigh, Littlebury, Little Maplestead, Saffron Walden, Stebbing, Thaxted, Waltham Abbey.

FENLAND.

113, 114. (Cambridge, Lincoln, Norfolk).

GLOUCESTER.

Ashchurch, Berkeley, Bristol, Chalcombe, Chipping Campden, Cirencester, Cotswolds, Deerhurst, Down Hatherley, Fairford, Frampton-on-Severn, Gloucester, Iron Acton, Northleach, Oxenhall, Sandhurst, Siston, Slimbridge, Tewkesbury, Tidenham, Winchcombe.

HAMPSHIRE.

Beaulieu, Christchurch, Corhampton, East Meon, Hurstbourne Priors, Romsey, St. Mary Bourne, Salisbury, Silchester, Southampton, Winchester.

HEREFORDSHIRE.

26, 114. Garway, Hereford, Ledbury, Leominster, Pembridge, Ross, Yarpole.

HERTFORDSHIRE.

St. Albans.

IRELAND.

32, 33, 52. The Dingle.

SOMERSET. 81, 107. Banwell, Barwick, Bristol, Congresbury, Croscombe, Dunster, Glastonbury, High Ham, Long Sutton, Minehead, Norton Fitzwarren, Porlock, Spaxton, Taunton, Templecombe, Trull, Wells, Wootton Courtney.

STAFFORDSHIRE. Lichfield, Rushton Spencer.

SUFFOLK. 100, 107. Beccles, Bury St. Edmunds, East Bergholt, Ipswich, Lavenham, Long Melford, Snape, Southwold, Sudbury, Theberton, Ufford, Wenhaston.

SURREY. 114. Cranleigh, Ockham, Southwark, Tandridge, Walton-on-the-Hill, West Horsley.

SUSSEX. Arundel, Bishopstone, Chichester, Edburton, Icklesham, Newhaven, New Shoreham, Old Shoreham, Parham, Playden, Pyecombe, Rye, Sompting, Steyning, Tangmere, Westham, Winchelsea, Worth.

WALES. 81. South, 107. Llanrhaiadr-y-Kinmerch, St. David's, Wrexham.

WARWICKSHIRE. Alveston, Billesley, Birmingham, Brownsover, Clifford Chambers, Coventry, Temple Balsall, Temple Grafton, Wootton Wawen, Wroxhall.

WEST OF ENGLAND. 58, 64, 77, 99, 107. (Cornwall, Devon, Gloucester, Hereford, Somerset).

WILTSHIRE. 81. Avebury, Bradford-on-Avon, Edington, Mere, Potterne, Salisbury.

WORCESTERSHIRE. Evesham, Longdon, Worcester.

YORKSHIRE. Barton-le-Street, Beverley, Fountains, Hackness, Hornsea, Hubberholme, Hull, Lastingham, Rievaulx, Ripon, Rotherham, Temple Newsom, Wakefield, Warmsworth, York.

Index of Subjects and Persons.

Barnicott and Pearce, The Wessex Press Taunton.

Lightning Source UK Ltd.
Milton Keynes UK
UKHW021829160223
417092UK00004B/290